EARLY ADOLESCENCE
TO EARLY ADULTHOOD

Volume 5, The Best of ACLD

EARLY ADOLESCENCE

Edited by

and

TO EARLY ADULTHOOD

Selected Papers from the 20th International Conference
of the Association for Children and Adults with Learning Disabilities

WILLIAM M. CRUICKSHANK, Ph.D.
School of Public Health
University of Michigan

JOANNE MARIE KLIEBHAN, O.S.F., Ph.D.
St. Francis Children's Activity and Achievement Center
Milwaukee, Wisconsin

SYRACUSE UNIVERSITY PRESS   1984

Library of Congress Cataloging in Publication Data
Association for Children and Adults with Learning
  Disabilities. International Conference (20th :
  1983 : Washington, D.C.)
  Early adolescence to early adulthood.

  (The Best of ACLD ; v. 5)
  Includes bibliographies.
  1. Learning disabilities—Congresses. I. Cruickshank,
William M. II. Kliebhan, Joanne Marie. III. Title.
IV. Series.
LC4704.A87 1983   371.9   83-17968
ISBN 0-8156-2301-1

Manufactured in the United States of America

CONTENTS

CONTRIBUTORS   vii

PREFACE   ix

ACLD EDITORIAL COMMITTEE FOR SELECTED
    PAPERS, 1983   xi

GENERAL OVERVIEWS
1 Prevention: Primary, Secondary, or Otherwise   3
    Rosa A. Hagin

2 ACLD-R&D Project Summary: A Study Investigating
    the Link between Learning Disabilities and Juvenile
    Delinquency   13
    Dorothy Crawford

3 Independent Living for Learning Disabled Adults:
    An Overview   19
    Carol Goodman, Dale Brown, Stephen Goodman,
    William Buffton

4 Social and Emotional Development of Learning
    Disabled Children   25
    Gloria H. Blanton

EDUCATIONAL AND SOCIAL TECHNIQUES
5 Coping Means Survival for Learning Disabled Adolescents   39
    Elaine Fine and Shirley Zeitlin

6 The Application of Study Techniques with Learning
    Disabled Adolescents   49
    Linda Mixon Clary

7 Beyond Academics: Programming for Young Learning
    Disabled Adults   61
    William C. Adamson, Dorothy Ohrenstein, Samuel Fiederer

8 Learning Disabilities and Social Skill Development: Research-
    Based Implications for the Developmental Life Span   69
    Paul J. Gerber and Rhonda H. Kelley

9 An Integrated System for Providing Content to Learning
Disabled Adolescents Using an Audio-Taped Format   79
Jean B. Schumaker, Donald D. Deshler, Pegi H. Denton

10 Group Screening for Language Learning Disabilities in
Junior High, High School, and Community College
Populations   109
Jacquelyn Gillespie

STEPS TO EMPLOYMENT

11 Seven Steps to Employment for Learning Disabled Students   117
Lloyd W. Tindall

12 A Neuropsychological Model for Vocational Planning for
Learning Disabled Students   143
Cathy F. Telzrow and Lawrence C. Hartlage

PROGRAMS FOR ADOLESCENTS

13 Denver Academy: A Program for Learning Disabled
Adolescents   157
Paul D. Knott and Stephan D. Tattum

14 The Barat College Writing Lab   177
Dee C. Konrad

Invited Paper: Background on the Canadian ACLD
Definition Adopted by CACLD, October 18, 1981   183
Barbara McElgunn

CONTRIBUTORS

WILLIAM C. ADAMSON, M.D., Clinical Professor of Child/Adolescent Psychiatry, Hahnemann Medical College and Hospital, Philadelphia, Pennsylvania

GLORIA H. BLANTON, Ph.D., School Psychologist III, Bladen County Schools, Elizabethtown, North Carolina

DALE BROWN, B.A., Program Manager, President's Committee on the Employment of the Handicapped, Washington, D.C.

WILLIAM BUFFTON, Director, Success Through Independent Living Program, New Jersey

LINDA MIXON CLARY, Ph.D. Assistant Professor, Augusta College, Augusta, Georgia

DOROTHY CRAWFORD, ACLD President, Scottsdale, Arizona

PEGI H. DENTON, University of Kansas Institute for Research in Learning Disabilities, Lawrence, Kansas

DONALD D. DESHLER, Ph.D., Director, University of Kansas Institute for Research in Learning Disabilities, Lawrence, Kansas

SAMUEL FIEDERER, M.A., Group Growth Services, Inc., Rydal, Pennsylvania

ELAINE FINE, Ph.D., Assistant Professor, Montclair State College, Upper Montclair, New Jersey

PAUL J. GERBER, Ph.D., Associate Professor of Special Education, University of New Orleans, New Orleans, Louisiana

JACQUELYN GILLESPIE, Assistant Professor, California Graduate Institute, Orange, California

CAROL GOODMAN, M.A., Co-Director, JESPY House, South Orange, New Jersey

STEPHEN GOODMAN, M.S.W., Co-Director, JESPY House, South Orange, New Jersey

ROSA A. HAGIN, Ph.D., Professor, Division of Psychological and Educational Services, Graduate School of Education, Fordham University, New York, New York

LAWRENCE C. HARTLAGE, Ph.D., Medical College of Georgia, Augusta, Georgia

RHONDA H. KELLEY, Doctoral Candidate, Department of Special Education, University of New Orleans, New Orleans, Louisiana

PAUL D. KNOTT, Ph.D., Executive Director, Denver Academy, Denver, Colorado

DEE C. KONRAD, Director, Communication Skills Program, Barat College, Lake Forest, Illinois

BARBARA McELGUNN, R.N., Chairman, National Research and Information Committee, Canadian Association for Children with Learning Disabilities

DOROTHY F. OHRENSTEIN, M.S.W., Group Growth Services, Inc., Rydal, Pennsylvania

JEAN B. SCHUMAKER, Ph.D., Coordinator of Research, University of Kansas Institute for Research in Learning Disabilities, Lawrence, Kansas

STEPHAN D. TATTUM, M.A., Program Director, Denver Academy, Denver, Colorado

CATHY F. TELZROW, Coordinator, Educational Assessment Project, Cuyahoga Special Education Service Center, Maple Heights, Ohio

LLOYD W. TINDALL, Project Associate, Vocational Studies Center, University of Wisconsin, Madison, Wisconsin

SHIRLEY ZEITLIN, Ph.D., Associate Professor, Montclair State College, Upper Montclair, New Jersey

PREFACE
From the Cradle To The Computer

AROUND THE MIDDLE of the twentieth century educators were beginning to accept the doctrine that infants and young children with behavioral, developmental, and learning disabilities *could* learn. Special educators started to work seriously on innovative curricula that could help preschool disabled children learn how to learn, regardless of their specific category of disability. Effective curricula and teaching strategies began to appear as a result of this new insight into the early learning potential of handicapped children.

Gradually, yesterday's learning disabled child became today's learning disabled adolescent, and the learning and social needs of teen-agers and young adults have opened new areas of investigation. Interest in how one learns has generated studies regarding process teaching, modality preferences, teaching to learning strengths or weaknesses, aptitude-treatment-interaction, direct instruction, task analysis, individual learning styles, and more. Controversial articles published in educational journals have been followed by heated rebuttals, leaving unanswered the question of *how one learns* open to future research.

Today, with the impact of the new electronic technology, "how one learns" has assumed equal importance with "how to teach" and "what to teach." The use of media in public school instruction has already modified educational technology. The emergent use of computers is revolutionizing the instructional system, with special emphasis on the learning disabled student. The total process of learning and teaching is being re-examined in terms of (1) specific objectives, (2) specific learning and communication needs of all children, and (3) specific teaching technologies available to meet the learning needs of each individual student.

The tools of instruction now extend beyond printed pages and audiovisual aids into the modern world of electronic communication.

The 1983 ACLD International Conference emphasized the role of computer technology in special education. We are at the threshold of major developments in the use of all media as instructional aids. Methods of instruction are being modified to a major degree, particularly in the presentation of information and the management of contingencies of reinforcement.

Ultimately a new kind of professional will be required to provide leadership in design, as well as implementation and evaluation of programs in education to maximize the use of the new electronic technology. This new educational "tech-pro" will be concerned with the basic task of analyzing problems in human learning and devising solutions to meet them. Improvements in educational technology will stem from the application of new communication methods to new concepts in learning theory.

This opens up an entirely new domain in educational research — a challenge to all of us concerned with the art of teaching, and particularly with teaching the learning disabled child and young adult. Both "how to teach" and "how one learns" are proper subjects for research. So is the need to develop software that will help students learn more and in less time. We are about to enter a brave new world of multi-media, multisensory instruction. ACLD provides a forum for the free and open exchange of theories, insights, and research findings as they emerge in our ongoing quest for the answers of how children learn!

For the Editorial Committee
Sister Joanne Marie Kliebhan, O.S.F., Ph.D.

ACLD EDITORIAL COMMITTEE
for Selected Papers
1983

xi

EARLY ADOLESCENCE
TO EARLY ADULTHOOD
Volume 5, The Best of ACLD

GENERAL OVERVIEWS

1

Prevention
Primary, Secondary, or Otherwise

Rosa A. Hagin

For the past dozen years my major professional interest has been in the prevention of learning failure and its emotional consequences. During these years of involvement in school based preventive projects, I have made some predictions and entertained some presumptions, although not necessarily in that order. It is the purpose of this paper to consider some of these ideas in the light of the hopeful, yet disconcerting field of prevention.

Our preventive projects have been located in schools of Community School District II on the east side of Manhattan. This district extends from Chinatown north to Yorkville, and from the East River west to Fifth Avenue — roughly the area served by Bellevue Psychiatric Hospital where the offices of the Learning Disorders Unit are located. In the course of these twelve years we have scanned intact samples of kindergarteners numbering 3,705 children. Intervention services, lasting generally two school years, have been provided to 935 children. Scanning, diagnosis, and intervention are done cooperatively, with Community School District II providing educational personnel and the Learning Disorders Unit providing clinical personnel. The small core staff of the Learning Disorders Unit is augmented by people who come to us for training. During these years we have trained (and exploited) 32 psychologists, 46 psychiatrists, 2 pediatricians, 4 medical students, 6 social workers, and 36 teachers.

In addition to these core projects in Community School District II, the Unit has provided training and continuing consultation to personnel in 151 schools serving 13,736 children through replications of our preventive approach. These projects are located in other New York City school districts, in suburban schools in the New York area, and in more distant schools as far north as Prince Edward Island, as far west as Hays, Kansas, as far south as Carrollton, Georgia, and as far east as New Bedford, Massachusetts.

This chapter will consider the field of prevention in general, as well as its specific applications to the field of learning disabilities. Ordinarily one starts such a task as this with a definition. A neat, popular one is "action to prevent the occurrence of a disease or disability in large populations" (Albee and Joffee 1977). A more classical definition from the field of public health divides preventive efforts into three parts: (1) *primary prevention* is used to refer to actions taken prior to the onset of a disease to intercept its causation or to modify its course; (2) *secondary prevention* is used to describe early diagnosis and treatment; (3) *tertiary prevention* is used to indicate rehabilitative efforts to reduce the residual effects of illness (Leavell and Clark 1965).

For example, primary prevention of mental retardation resulting from errors in amino acid metabolism, such as phenylketonuria, could be directed toward identifying the carrier of this defect and offering genetic counseling to the family, while secondary prevention would provide nutritional services to the child and clinical counseling to help the family to maintain the affected youngster on the phenylalanine-restricted diet. Tertiary prevention would provide educational and vocational services to enable the PKU child to utilize his/her abilities most effectively.

However, the neat stages of primary-secondary-tertiary prevention are more appropriate where research has established a more nearly linear cause and effect relationship between toxic agents and the condition one is attempting to prevent. When making predictions about educational outcomes, one must take into account not only the children's individual patterns of development, but also the environmental supports and stresses they experience, the match between the child and the learning environment. It is not so much a matter of discovering and correcting what is wrong within the children, but rather of learning to understand and to deal effectively with the complex array of forces and feedback loops that influences the quality of their lives. This diversity would give pause to even the most courageous investigator, for it is not easy to apply the principles of prevention to conditions such as learning failure which are multiply-determined and multiply-defined. Therefore, I ask you to consider yet another definition of prevention provided by a sensible, if somewhat inarticulate youngster in response to item 15 on the Vocabulary subtest of the Wechsler Intelligence Scale for Children-Revised: "prevent means to make something not happen."

Prevention is an appealing concept. Few people would admit to being opposed; in fact, most people feel that they are already working at it. In a sense they are. As Kessler and Albee (1977) concluded in their review of primary prevention research, practically every effort aimed at improving the human condition can be considered part of primary prevention. As a corollary, it would seem that anything done to improve the quality of education would be regarded as contributing to the prevention of learning failure. However, the body of evidence from the field does not support the belief that global approaches serve the course of prevention as effectively as *specific* programs based on *specific* formulations of the conditions one is attempting to prevent (Erlenmeyer-Kimling 1977).

SOME JUSTIFICATIONS

Compared with intervention after the child has failed, prevention is not only possible, it is cheaper and better for the mental health of the children and their families. For example, Fitzsimmons, Cheever, Leonard and Macunovich (1969) found in a retrospective study of high school drop-outs and poorly performing graduates that signs of learning failure were apparent early in their schooling. In their sample, 50 percent of the school failures were already identifiable by second grade, 75 percent by fourth grade, and 90 percent by seventh grade. These investigators noted patterns of spreading failure as the children moved through the grades. Early failure in skill subjects (reading first, then mathematics) spread to content subjects as well. These investigators concluded that general communication skills are vital to consequent success in other academic areas.

While the Fitzsimmons *et al.* study showed that it is possible to identify potential drop-outs and poor achievers early, an experiment by Bry and George (1980) demonstrated that it is feasible to apply preventive approaches even as late as junior high school. They provided a counseling program which fed back to students the results of teacher evaluations and attendance data. They concluded that the "special attention of a firm, consistent adult" resulted in significant differences favoring the experimental group in both grades and attendance. The fact that these differences did not appear until the program had been in operation for two years provides an important lesson in patience for those who would work in prevention.

Prevention would also appear to make sense financially, although it is difficult to compute the cost of something that you have made "not happen." One could, of course, look to the costs of special education as an alternative provision for children who have failed to learn. And an expensive alternative it is! Estimates of costs for several kinds of provisions for children after they have failed to learn in regular school classes have been computed on a per-pupil basis for instructional costs only. These estimates do not include costs of referral, diagnosis, individual educational planning, classification meetings, and due process hearings.

The first setting is a resource room which provides small group and individual instruction to learning disabled children as a supplement to regular classroom instruction. The cost for this service is approximately $1500 per child. Because the children also continue to be enrolled in regular classrooms for the rest of the day, this figure must be added to the per-pupil cost for regular classroom instruction, yielding a total of $3000 per child for resource room services.

A self-contained class provides limited enrollments of ten pupils for children who need the structure of such a classroom. Costs for a special education teacher, materials, coverage, supervision, and pupil transportation for an estimated 70 percent of the pupils bring the per-pupil cost for this service to $3900.

A second kind of self-contained class with more auxiliary services for children with both emotional and learning problems is estimated to have a per-pupil cost of $5100. Tuitions for independent schools for learning disabled children vary widely, but the figure of $7,000 (plus transportation costs) represents a very moderate estimate. Thus, after children have failed, instructional costs range from three to more than seven thousand dollars per pupil.

In contrast, instructional costs for our school-based preventive program are $656 during the first year and $472 for the second year. These costs, added to the regular per-pupil cost of $1500, total $2186 and $1972 for the first and second years respectively. Included in these estimates are teachers' salaries, supervision, materials, and support services during the first year of the program, with the addition of an educational assistant during the second and continuing years of the program.

While it is to be expected that a variety of educational provisions must be made for children with special learning needs, prudent educational planning would lead one to consider the inclusion of preventive approaches among these alternatives. Sound mental health principles would also advise consideration of preventive programs. The report of the Task Panel on Learning Failure and Unused Learning Potential, submitted to the President's Commission on Mental Health in 1978, documented the effect of learning failure on the quality of family life and community mental health. This report made a strong case for prevention with the statement, "Early identification and intervention is critical if the child is to avoid failure, shame, and the conviction of self-blame andworthlessness" (Bryant 1978).

BARRIERS TO PREVENTION

How is it then that a concept that is so appealing, inexpensive, feasible, and mentally healthy has not won universal acceptance? What are the barriers to implementation of preventive approaches? It is not just the fact that present joys are more alluring than distant good, nor the lack of a vocal constituency to demand preventive action. If it were, I might consider going around with a piece of chalk so that I could write "Push Prevention!" on the walls alongside such slogans as "No Nukes" or "Save the whales!" Nor do I think that it necessarily results from the way educational services are funded, although it *does* appear that our government gives strong legal and financial encouragement to persuade school districts to establish provisions for children after they have failed to learn.

Real barriers to prevention appear in the natural resistance to change. Prevention on any broad scale, whatever the target, presents a threat to the *status quo*. The prospect of general uncertainty and personal insecurity implicit in change is not usually a comfortable one. Most of us do not welcome the opportunity to put ourselves out of business. Entrenched, self-centered thinking can blunt the effects of the brightest new insights. Furthermore, preventive approaches also present a threat to privacy and individual rights. You would be well aware of this if you have ever encountered the smoker who finds himself seated in the non-smoking section of an airplane.

In contrast to the rigid thinking that tries to preserve things as they are, we have the manic idealism that will not be satisfied with less than a perfect world. There is a common misconception that little can be accomplished, short of a major overhaul of all society's institutions. Some people will not settle for half-way measures. They believe that prevention can occur only when it has been possible to abolish economic insecurity, social injustice, poverty, slums, illness, war, child abuse, pollution — in short, until we have the capacity to right all that is wrong with our world. While these intentions may be admirable and the causes just, such all-or-nothing thinking does not serve the cause of prevention well, for it only results in delay, inaction, and disappointment.

Another barrier to prevention is the difficulty in documenting results. It is not easy to demonstrate to yourself and others that you have made something "not happen." One may agree with Flanagan (1971) that progress in improving human behavior is only possible if research data are evaluated and validated in such a way as to permit sound conclusions. However, it is not easy to maintain the conditions for valid research in the real world of the schools.

Broskowski and Baker (1974) have questioned whether traditional research methodologies, with their use of control groups, manipulation of multiple variables, and statistical analyses with the assumptions of random sampling, are appropriate to cope with the complexities of research in prevention. Evaluation of preventive approaches must provide for the multiple goals, unanticipated conditions (both positive and negative) and ethical considerations, such as withholding of treatment to preserve a control condition or diffusion effects that can afflict multiple cohort designs. Most important of all, these designs must provide adequate time to observe the outcomes of the experimental predictions and interventions. All of this requires us to reconcile the conditions for valid research and evaluation with the conditions in which our work is done.

LEARNING DISORDERS UNIT MODEL

Despite the barriers to prevention such as resistance to change, inadequate funding, and difficulty in documenting results, the Learning Disorders Unit has continued its preventive work. Our model, developed over a period of twelve years, provides (1) scanning intact samples of kindergarten children to identify those who are vulnerable to learning failure (2) diagnosis to determine, if possible, the reasons for their vulnerability (3) educational intervention to build the neuropsychological skills necessary for learning. This model was refined and replicated through funding as a Child Service Demonstration Center by the Bureau of Education for the Handicapped during 1976–79. In September, 1979 our submission to the Joint Dissemination Review Panel of the U.S. Department of Education and the National Institute of Education was approved unanimously. This approval was based on the panel's judgment of statistical evaluation of the model program's educational impact, replicability, and cost effectiveness.

While the need for continued research in primary prevention is acknowledged, our efforts have been directed toward secondary prevention — that is, finding children at risk for learning failure who have not yet failed. The initial step in secondary prevention is to identify the precursors of failure.

Our search for precursors has led us to hypothesize that, underlying the multiple clinical pictures of vulnerable children, there is one common characteristic: immaturity in spatial orientation and temporal organization. This *anlage* may be found in young, vulnerable children, regardless of the etiology of that vulnerability. Thus, it may be seen in the various subgroups of children who comprise the heterogeneous group of learning failures: children with specific language disability, children with dysfunction or deficit of the central nervous system, or children who have had discordant neuroperceptual input at critical ages for language development. This formulation has its basis in both experimental and clinical data (Silver & Hagin, 1964; Silver & Hagin, 1965). A ten-year follow-up study found that neuropsychological deficits, present during childhood, persisted into adulthood almost unchanged. Moreover, there was an association between reading retardation and the persistence of these deficits. Our interest in prevention led us to assess the utility of this association in prediction. Would the failure to develop age-appropriate skills in spatial orientation and temporal organization signal vulnerability to learning problems in young children?

This question was explored in a clinical study of 169 children, all those with birth dates during 1963 and 1964 enrolled in the first grades of one New York City public school. Our criterion for the prediction of learning failure was the presence of deviations in spatial orientation and temporal organization. These deviations were found in approximately 20 percent of the children in the intact groups we studied. A follow-up study of the entire class using oral reading and reading comprehension test scores as criteria showed that, by the end of fourth grade, predictions based on our clinical examination were accurate to within 1 percent of false positives and 5 percent false negatives (Hagin and Silver 1977).

With these studies as a background, attempt was made to reduce the lengthy clinical examinations to a reliable and valid scanning measure. Factor analysis of the twenty variables of the clinical examination defined five factors, showing the independence of the auditory and visual factors from each other, as well as from emotional and cognitive variables, and from chronological age. Loadings within factors helped locate the measures which most clearly defined each component of the scanning test, which we called SEARCH (Silver & Hagin 1976).

SEARCH emerged as a twenty-minute individual test, designed to be given in kindergarten or early in first grade. It consists of ten components, the raw scores of which may be evaluated by either age or local norms. The results of SEARCH provide a total score to predict vulnerability to learning failure and a profile of strengths and needs to guide educational intervention (Silver & Hagin 1976).

How accurate are these predictions? *False negatives* identified children for whom normal learning progress was predicted, but who did not achieve well. Using grade expectancy achievement in reading as a criterion, we found the incidence of false negatives to be 8 percent at the end of first grade, and 4 percent at the end of second and third grades for 1,069 children studied. *False positives* (children for whom the test predicts failure and who did not fail) are more difficult to locate than false negatives, because our program usually intervenes with vulnerable children in the core schools. However, there were three schools in which the intervention program had not yet been introduced, or where there was insufficient teacher time in the resource room. The 133 children from this sample received instruction in accordance with the regular school curriculum. Using grade expectancy in reading as a criterion, again, we found false positives ranging from 0 to 9 percent in these schools.

The validity and utility of SEARCH has also been assessed in terms of the diagnostic examination in a study in which 171 children (B.D. 1967), comprising the total first grade of two schools, were seen for clinical study. When SEARCH score grouping (based on a range from 0 to 10) were charted against clinical diagnoses, some characteristic trends emerged. Of the 22 children who earned SEARCH scores within the 0–3 group, 19 demonstrated pervasive biological problems: chronic illness, mental retardation, and positive findings on neurological examinations. Of the 37 children earning SEARCH scores of 4 and 5, 23 were found to have specific language disabilities. Approximately half of the children earning SEARCH scores of 6 and 7 had emotional problems or were reacting to family disorganization. Of the 69 children earning SEARCH scores of 8–10, no deviations on the clinical examinations were found in 61. SEARCH scores, therefore, while not in any way a substitute for intensive clinical study, can suggest priorities in the allocation of scarce diagnostic services and can guide intervention services as well.

The third part of the model, our educational intervention, approach has been described elsewhere (TEACH, Hagin, Silver, and Kreeger 1976; *Journal of Learning Disabilities;* Hagin, Silver, and Beecher 1978). What is relevant here is the variety of methods by which it has been assessed:

1. The Joint Dissemination Review Panel submission used data from B.D. 1970 for analysis of variance with a control group design comparing "intervention" with "no intervention" and data from B.D. 1971 in a two-cohort design that contrasted "more" and "less" intervention. All differences favored program participants.
2. A follow-up study at fifth grade, utilizing unobtrusive measures, showed that intervention group children were not distinguishable from their classmates (for whom normal learning progress had been predicted) on measures of motivation for school learning and interpersonal relationships.
3. An independent replication done by a group of investigators in Columbus, Ohio public schools found at the end of the project and on follow-up one year later that the TEACH group differed significantly from an academic tutoring group and a no-contact controls on perceptual skills, reading achievement, and behavior ratings. (Arnold *et al.* 1977)

We have learned a number of lessons in the school-based preventive programs:

1. Early identification programs must be reviewed in relation to the learning ecology. For this reason we prefer the term "scanning" (i.e., viewing the educational configuration) to "screening," which implies illness within the child that makes him or her unacceptable in the educational setting.
2. Vulnerability to learning problems is a many-splendored thing. Even at

the early age of six years, diagnostic studies show that these children do not represent a homogeneous group. It is this multidimensionality that invites confusion, frustration, and failure of replication in research. One cannot assume that the problems associated with learning failure in one child are the same as those in every other child who fails to learn. In reality, within this group of children, there are marked individual differences in functioning and in assets and deficits. The importance of these variations is that, in any study of large numbers of children, these individual differences may cancel each other out. The consequent balancing effect may cause an unwary investigator to dismiss as unimportant some variables that may be crucial to some of the children in the sample.

3. Our work with intact samples has dispelled some of the myths that have entered our field by way of the biases implicit in research done with referred samples. Referred samples of children with learning disabilities usually have a disproportionately large number of boys. Our intact samples of young children, year after year, yield a virtually equal number of vulnerable boys and girls. We also find that incidence of vulnerability is generally proportional to the ethnic representation in the total sample. The one exception is that the schools with a high proportion of Chinese children tend to have high scores on the visual perception components of SEARCH — but that is the beginning of another paper.

There are also some non-quantitative lessons. We have learned to take risks with children who earn low scores on intelligence tests — we find considerably fewer truly retarded children in our intact samples than we had been taught to expect. Although I could not write down this criteria exactly, we have learned to assess the climate of a school in terms of its readiness for change — and to plan our replications appropriately. We have also learned that effective prevention is an interdisciplinary job, and have grown in mutual understanding and respect as we have worked in schools with our non-clinical colleagues. Finally, we have learned that preventive approaches have much to contribute to the education of young children.

REFERENCES

Albee, J. W., and J. M. Joffe. *Primary Prevention of Psychopathology*. Hanover, N.H.: University Press of New England, 1977.

Arnold, E. E., N. Barneby, J. McManus, D. J. Smetzer. "Prevention by Specific Remediation for Vulnerable First Graders." *Archives of General Psychiatry* 34 (1977): 1279–1293.

Bry, B. H., and F. E. George. "The Preventive Effects of Early Intervention on the Attendance and Grades of Urban Adolescents." *Professional Psychology* 11 (1980): 252–260.

Bryant, T. E. "The Effect of Student Failure on the Quality of Family Life and Community Mental Health." *Bulletin of the Orton Society* 28 (1978): 8–14.

Erlenmeyer-Kimling, L. "Issues Pertaining to Prevention and Intervention of Genetic Disorders Affecting Human Behavior." J. W. Albee and J. M. Joffee, eds., *Primary Prevention of Psychopathology.* Hanover, N.H.: University Press of New England, 1977.

Fitzsimmons, S. J., J. Cheever, E. Leonard, and D. Macunovich. "School Failures: Now and Tomorrow." *Developmental Psychology* 1 (1969): 134–147.

Flanagan, J. "Evaluation and Validation of Research Data in Primary Prevention." *American Journal of Orthopsychiatry* 41 (1971): 117–124.

Hagin, R. A., and A. A. Silver. "Learning Disability: Definition, Diagnosis, and Prevention." *New York University Education Quarterly* 8 (1977): 9–16.

Hagin, R. A., A. A. Silver, and H. Kreeger. *"TEACH: Learning Tasks for the Prevention of Learning Disability."* New York: Walker Educational Book Corporation, 1976.

Keesler, M., and G. W. Albee. "An Overview of the Literature of Primary Prevention." J. W. Albee and J. M. Joffee, eds. *Primary Prevention of Psychopathology.* Hanover, N.H.: University Press of New England, 1977.

Leavell, H. R., and E. G. Clark. *Preventive Medicine for the Doctor in his Community.* New York: McGraw-Hill, 1965.

Silver, A. A., and R. A. Hagin. "Specific Reading Disability: Follow-up Studies." *American Journal of Orthopsychiatry* 34 (1964): 95–102.

Silver, A. A., and R. A. Hagin. "Developmental Language Disability Simulating Mental Retardation." *Journal of the Academy of Child Psychiatry* 4 (1965): 485–493.

Silver, A. A., and R. A. Hagin. *"SEARCH: A Scanning Instrument for the Identification of Potential Learning Disability."* New York: Walker Educational Book Corporation, 1976.

Silver, A. A., R. A. Hagin, and R. Beecher. "Scanning, Diagnosis, and Intervention in the Prevention of Reading Disabilities." *Journal of Learning Disabilities* 11 (1978): 437–449.

2

ACLD-R&D Project Summary
A Study Investigating the Link between Learning Disabilities and Juvenile Delinquency

Dorothy Crawford

THIS SUMMARY is in three parts: (1) capsuled historical overview of the reason for and purpose of the study; (2) highlights of the study's results; and (3) recommendations or conclusions.

HISTORY

The issue of a possible link between learning disabilities and juvenile delinquency surfaced in the late 1960s and early 1970s.

The National Institute for Juvenile Justice and Delinquency Prevention responded in 1975 to this increased interest and concern in learning disabilities and juvenile delinquency. They had Dr. Charles Murray, American Institutes for Research, commissioned to evaluate current theory and knowledge relevant to the proposition that learning disabilities increase the risk of becoming delinquent and to make policy recommendations. Murray, after reviewing the hard evidence that had been gathered through 1975, concluded that previous research was so inconclusive that it could not be used (to quote Murray) "even for rough estimates of the strength of the link." His report recommended that carefully controlled investigations be conducted to determine the effects of learning disabilities on delinquency. Also, that an academic remediation program be designed, implemented and conducted and evaluated to assess the effects of diagnosing and treating delinquents with learning disabilities. Similar conclusions and recommendations were reached in a study conducted by the GAO about the same time.

Supported by Grant Numbers 76-JN-99-0021 and 78-JN-AX-0022 from the National Institute for Juvenile Justice and Delinquency Prevention, Office of Juvenile Justice and Delinquency Prevention, Law Enforcement Assistance Administration, U. S. Department of Justice. Points of view or opinions in this paper are those of the author and do not represent the official position or policies of the U.S. Department of Justice.

In 1976 NIJJDP funded the R&D study, the purpose of which was to establish reliable data that would assist in a methodical development of informed policy and programs. One grant was awarded to the Association for Children with Learning Disabilities (ACLD) to *design and conduct a remediation program for LD juvenile delinquents, to improve academic skills, change school attitudes and reduce the delinquency of LD teenagers who had been officially adjudicated as delinquents by a juvenile court.* A second grant was awarded to the National Center for State Courts (NCSC) to *undertake investigations of the relationship, if any, between learning disabilities and juvenile delinquency and to conduct an evaluation of the effectiveness of the ACLD remediation program.*

HIGHLIGHTS OF THE RESULTS

Note: The designs of both the research and development components were *carefully planned* with *special precautions* taken to *insure valid and reliable data.*

Research

1. The evidence for the existence of a relationship between learning disabilities and self-reported delinquency was statistically significant.
2. LD adolescents reported a *significantly higher frequency of violent acts.*
3. LD was *strongly related to official delinquency.* The *probability* of being officially delinquent (on a national measure) was *9* of every *100 LD adolescent males* compared to *4* of every *100 non-LD adolescent males.* To put it even more dramatically: the odds of being adjudicated delinquent were 220 percent greater for adolescents with learning disabilities than for their non-LD peers!
4. The same odds ratio applied for being taken into custody by the police.
5. The incidence of LD in the adjudicated delinquent group was 36 percent. This indicates that a substantial proportion of official delinquents are handicapped with LD.

These data alone indicate LD youths as a high risk group of adolescents in need of special services. They are a population who are *relatively* at higher risk than their non-LD counterparts. The comparative basis is what gives us reason for concern.

6. The *greater delinquency* of LD youths *could not be attributed to socio-demographic characteristics* or a *tendency to disclose socially disapproved behaviors.*
7. The data indicated that *LD contributed to increases of delinquent behavior* both directly and indirectly *through school failure.*
8. For *comparable offenses LD juveniles* had *higher probabilities of arrest* and *adjudication* than those *without LD.*
9. Among adjudicated delinquents there was no difference between those LD and non-LD for being incarcerated.
10. As *officially non-delinquent boys advance* through their *teens, those with LD experience greater increases in delinquent activities.*

Finally, while only a *relatively small proportion of the youth population is affected by LD, LD appears to be one of the important causes of delinquency.*

Remediation Program Results

1. There was *significant improvement in intellectual growth with 55 to 65 hours of remedial instruction in one school year.*
2. There was a *dramatic decrease in delinquency* with at *least 40–50* hours of instruction. The *instruction was significantly effective* in *preventing* or *controlling future delinquency.*
3. A major factor in preventing delinquency was *not* academic skills improvement but seemed to be *due* to the *nature of the relationship between the adolescents and the LD specialists.*
4. The model of instruction did *significantly provide academic/intellectual growth* and *reduce delinquent acitivity;* it *did not statistically change school attitudes.*

RECOMMENDATIONS

The following recommendations are made on the basis of (1) the results of the R&D study; (2) initiatives that should or could be conducted at state and local levels; and (3) consideration of social and economic cost effectiveness.

Although additional research is certainly needed, it is recommended that the present findings, in combination with the other research done to date, be used to guide the formulation of juvenile justice and educational policy. We believe that our research provides a sound basis for informed action.

The findings demonstrate that adolescents handicapped by learning disabilities are a high-risk group for delinquency. This implies that juvenile justice, human services, and educational agencies should target special prevention and rehabilitation programs for this population. Some rehabilitation programs such as our remediation program and Project New Pride have proven effective in remediating academic deficiencies and reducing future delinquency. The availability of such rehabilitation services should be expanded. Most practitioners and researchers believe that it is important to identify and offer special services to learning-disabled children before they become official delinquents; that is, while they are still at an early age. Although there is no firm evidence to support this contention, such a prevention strategy for predelinquent learning-disabled children is reasonable enough to warrant implementation and evaluation.

Learning disabled youths' relatively greater probability of arrest and adjudication for offenses comparable to those of non-learning disabled teenagers suggests that special court services may be needed to offset the disadvantages suffered by this handicapped group. Training programs on the difficulties confronted by learning-disabled youths in the juvenile justice system could be helpful in augmenting the skills of police and probation officers, prosecutors, defense attorneys, and judges to deal effectively with this group of youthful offenders. Thoughtful consideration ought to be given to special court procedures for handling learning disabled youths. Recently several of these have been proposed or adopted in some courts.

We must have a major stimulus to local agencies to implement programs. An initiative on the national level could be very effective in stimulating state and local juvenile courts, correctional institutions, and educational agencies to offer remedial services for learning disabled delinquents and predelinquents. A public awareness campaign should be mounted to provide information to the general public about the potential need for and benefits of delinquency prevention and control among children with LD. More importantly, research results and recommendations should be disseminated to federal, state and local organizations that serve learning disabled youth. Interest and commitment will have to be developed at the community level in order for the necessary resources to be allocated to providing prevention and rehabilitation services for learning disabled children and youth.

Once communities have become interested in and expressed a desire to create such prevention and rehabilitation services, they will be immediately confronted by the problem of how to implement and efficiently operate these programs. Information and training needs to be made available to local agencies concerning curriculum materials; teacher training; LD assessment; program management; public awareness programs; models for implementing the remedial instruction design in schools, alternative educational programs, correctional facilities, and youth service agencies; approaches to coordinating the resources and demands of the juvenile courts, schools, and other agencies; ideas for revising juvenile justice procedures (e.g., forms) to promote fair treatment of learning disabled teenagers who have been taken into police custody; and a host of related issues.

There are obvious needs for procedures manuals on LD assessment, local program evaluation, and program monitoring to identify subgroups not benefitting maximally from the remedial services.

One of the greatest needs that will be confronted by local program planners will involve creating organizational and management plans that will promote coordination of effort by local agencies. Local efforts could be aided immensely if program models for the coordination of juvenile justice, educational, and youth services agencies were available to them.

At the federal level, we need practical research, program development, training and technical assistance and information dissemination.

In common ordinary terms, to implement these recommendations is cheap insurance.

3

Independent Living for
Learning Disabled Adults
An Overview

Carol Goodman, Dale Brown,
Stephen Goodman, William Buffton

U NTIL THE MID-1960s, the field of special education barely recognized the learning disabled. It is only in the past 20 years that there has been such growth in acceptance of this entity. With that acceptance has come a range of services, programs, research, legislation, and a group of special educators with specific expertise in working with this population.

For those young adults who are now over 20, however, there has been a common history of early disappointments, failures, and misunderstanding. Their "hidden handicap" went unrecognized not only by them but by the educators and other professionals who provided services to them. We are faced today with a group of learning disabled adults about whom we know little and for whom we know not what to do. Only recently has the field itself come to acknowledge that a learning disability is not always outgrown (Osman 1982).

The literature contains a wealth of material about the school-age and preschool age child, but contains few studies which truly research the learning disabled adult. Those studies which are available contain designs in which the parameters are too narrow, too broad, where diagnosis is made retrospectively, or where findings are inconclusive. The recent surveys of young adults conducted by White et al. (1980) and the ACLD Vocational Committee (1982) evaluate this population, yet they lead one to draw few substantive conclusions.

Similarly, the range of services available to the learning disabled, as seen in the types of remediation materials as well as a survey of the programs nationwide demonstrate the overwhelming bias towards the school age child.

Therefore, one wonders what has become of this group of young people who have completed their formal schooling. School experiences were by and large incomplete both in terms of academic preparation and in socialization. Family experiences often ran the gamut of overprotection, re-

19

jection, or general overinvolvement. In their desire to find out what was wrong and to seek the best treatment, these young adults have been over-evaluated and have been to see just about every new educational expert or therapist who promised the cure. Through all of this, these young people escaped doing their share of household chores, missed out on the important experience of being part of a peer group, and misperceived their power to move the world (based on their power to move their family). In short, these learning disabled young adults are ill-prepared for autonomous functioning in the community.

Programs for this population have begun to appear in the last 10 years. There are post-secondary programs for those with specific learning disabilities who can handle a college curriculum with tutoring and other supportive services.

There is, however, one group of learning disabled who have more severe impairments and are unable to handle this type of program. This group is also ill-prepared for independent living without further training. They generally have several kinds of impairments (such as cerebral palsy, perceptual handicaps, speech defects), more overt soft neurological signs, and emotional overlay secondary to the organic impairment. For this group, a residential setting is the appropriate avenue.

Across the country, there are now four centers of independent living, with several more in the planning stages (Brown 1982). Although there is very little information published as yet, those involved in delivery of these services recognize the need for more programs as well as more information on the teaching of life skills.

This paper will present some common characteristics of these programs and a rationale for including these services.

A MODEL FOR DELIVERY OF SERVICES

Although each program reflects the philosophy, training, and style of its administrators and program planners, the types of skills taught remain constant: vocational skills, life skills, social skills and emotional development. It is also to be noted that the emphasis placed on learning each skill might differ.

Vocational Skills

Each program acknowledges the importance of finding an appropriate job for the resident as well as teaching that individual how to keep the job. The young adult who enters the program of independent living often has very little information about his/her strengths and weaknesses, and equally little experience in the world of work.

With the aid of vocational counselors on staff and at the state level (in the state's vocational rehabilitation office), the young adult receives a vocational assessment and participates in development of a vocational plan. If the young person is work-ready, they are geared for a job placement. If the young person needs skills, or needs to work on inappropriate behaviors that would negatively effect their job performance, they would be referred to a sheltered workshop for behavior modification.

After completing such training, which would include job-seeking skills (application filing, dress, interview skills, etc.), a job placement is secured. Some programs have a job developer whose mission it is to develop the leads and contacts. Once a placement is made, there is need to constantly monitor and intervene for the young adult, the supervisor, and the co-workers. The young adult's poor judgment and impulsivity or low productivity may make them poor risks for long-term employment. Yet with intervention and education of the employer, the young adult can successfully maintain employment.

Most programs require a reasonable length of employment before community living is arranged.

Life Skills

Activities of daily living, or life skills, form another important part of the residential services. Because these young adults have come from sheltered home experiences or residential school settings, their exposure to household chores is minimal. With task analyses of all the chores of apartment maintenance (cooking, cleaning, menu preparation, marketing, and washing dishes) and self-maintenance (budgeting, grooming, hygiene, travel training) the staff teaches these young adults all aspects of daily living. Although the specific approach may differ, these residential programs all have very practical methods whereby the individual is taught by doing the chores with supervision. A reasonable level of skills must be accomplished for independent living.

Social Skills and Emotional Development

Learning disabled adults who fall within this range of impairment are characterized by social inappropriateness. They misperceive social cues, have difficulty forming and sustaining relationships, and have not learned the 'rules' of socializing. Despite their chronological age, they tend to function on an early adolescent level, displaying the behavior of that age. Early experiences reflect their rejection by their peers, and many learned to accept the role of the outcast with either an aggressive or passive-aggressive stance.

Task analyses of social skills enable staff to teach appropriate behaviors formally in groups, or informally on an ongoing basis. Techniques utilized include role playing, modeling, group process, and videotape. In some settings, individual and group counseling facilitates emotional exploration and growth. Family ties often become an area of concern, where the family has difficulty allowing the young person to individuate. Family therapy becomes a useful tool for establishing appropriate boundaries and for re-organizing the family structure to allow the young person to leave home.

The group living situation provides a unique opportunity to participate in a built-in peer group. Experiencing this for the first time, this social group has enormous power to teach about sharing, conflict resolution, and relationships. Birthdays, joys, and sorrows are experienced in a new fashion as the residents learn about living in society.

Each program also facilitates social skills via rules and limits. With varying degrees of structure, residents are taught explicitly about what is allowed and what is not. This also represents a unique opportunity to prepare for independent functioning in the community.

A reasonable level of social appropriateness, maturity, judgment and initiative is achieved before plans are made to move into the community.

SUMMARY AND CONCLUSIONS

Residential centers for independent living have begun to appear in the last 10 years, specifically geared to teach the learning disabled young adult how to live on his/her own. Key areas for autonomous functioning have been identified: social skills, vocational skills, and life skills.

Group living programs provide services that are necessary for these severely learning disabled adults. A residential setting is ideal for this group who are so ill-prepared for independent living and who have never lived away from their families. The group setting is ideal because: (1) it provides a built-in peer group; (2) around-the-clock guidance is available and offers the opportunity to accomplish more than is feasible in a once-a-week therapy session; and (3) living in a group teaches one about living in society.

REFERENCES

ACLD Vocational Committee. "Report on LD Adult." *ACLD Newsbriefs* (Sept/ Oct 1982).

Brown, Dale. *Steps to Independence for People with Learning Disabilities.* Washington, D.C.: Closer Look, 1980.

_____. "Independent Living & Learning Disabled Adults." *American Rehabilitation* 7, No. 6 (July/August 1982).

Hardy, M. I. "Disabled Readers: What Happens to Them after Elementary School?" *Canadian Education and Research Digest* 8 (1968).

Huessey, H., and A. Cohen. "Hyperkinetic Behaviors and Learning Disabilities Followed over Seven Years." *Pediatrics* 57 (1976).

Hunter, E., and H. M. Lewis. "Dyslexic Child—Two Years Later." *Journal of Psychology* 83 (1973).

Lehtinen, H., and J. Tuomisto. "On the Construction and Application of an Activation Variable in the Planning of Adult Education Systems." *Adult Education in Finland* 13 (1976).

Mankes, M., J. Rowe, and J. Menkes. "A 25-Year Follow-up Study on the Hyperkinetic Child with MBD." *Pediatrics* 39 (1967).

Myers, Patricia, and Donald Hammill. *Learning Disabilities: Basic Concepts, Assessment, Practices & Instructional Strategies.* Austin, Tex.: Pro-Ed, 1982.

Osman, Betty, and Henriette Blinder. *No One to Play With.* New York: Random House, 1982.

Rawson, M. *Developmental Language Disability: Adult Accomplishment of Dyslexic Boys.* Baltimore, Md.: Johns Hopkins University Press, 1968.

Reiss, A. J., with O. D. Duncan, P. K. Hatt, and C. C. North. *Occupations and Social Status.* Glencoe: The Free Press, 1961.

White, Warren J., J. B. Schumaker, M. M. Warner, G. R. Alley, and D. D. Deshler. "The Current Status of Young Adults Identified as Learning Disabled During their School Career." Institute for Research in Learning Disabilities, University of Kansas, January 1980.

4

Social and Emotional Development of Learning Disabled Children

Gloria H. Blanton

Many of us share with Kronick the conclusion that, in spite of academic remediation, many learning disabled children exhibit "a quality of social inepititude and imperviousness" (1981, p. ix) which is not explained by secondary emotional problems or experiences related to academic difficulties. As far back as Alfred Strauss' studies in the 1940s the literature about children labeled with minimal brain dysfunction — or specific learning disabled as we now identify them in educational circles — were considered emotionally labile. Johnson and Myklebust, Ernest Siegal, William M. Cruickshank, and other leaders in the field associate deficits in social perception with neurological learning disorders.

Some children have combinations of academic disabilities, inattention and impulsivity, and socioemotional problems. Most LD children are likely to have difficulty with all stages of psycho-social development and the mastery of developmental tasks. Social and emotional stresses are intensified for the estimated 40 percent who are hyperactive and distractible.

Two — if not more — findings from recent research should motivate us to be more concerned about increasing our emphasis on social and emotional change along with academic remediation. One is the probability that greater academic gains occur when adequate attention is given to those aspects of students' functioning (Cartledge and Milburn 1978). Another is the finding that the odds of being taken into custody by the police and "being adjudicated delinquent were 220 percent greater for adolescents with learning disabilities than for their non-learning disabled peers" according to the 1976 ACLD Research and Development Project (ACLD, *ACLD NEWSBRIEFS,* Mar./Apr. 1982).

It is urgent that individual education plans (IEPs) and other therapeutic and remediation efforts help children with their social and emotional needs because the very nature of children's profiles of strengths and disabilities means they are inclined to have problems. In addition, the failures, frustrations, criticisms, rejections and sometimes the ridicule, contribute to the probability that secondary emotional problems will develop unless they receive substantial special attention to help avoid them.

Adequate assessment is a crucial prerequisite to the development of comprehensive IEPs. Socio-emotional behavioral characteristics are an essential data component in an adequate psycho-educational assessment. Information can be gathered by use of rating scales, behavioral analysis, projective techniques and other measures to identify problem behaviors and attitudes which interfere with or reduce attainment of curricular objectives.

Consider Steven's embarrassment following laughter and strange looks from others after someone said, "How are you today?" and he replied, "I'm 10 years old but today is NOT my birthday!" Or think of Hugh who, upon being sent to the principal's office for lying, walked behind the desk within inches of the authority figure and giggled when the principal asked him why he did it. Or think for a moment of a child you know well. How does one's difficulty determining left and right and orienting one's self in space or difficulty with depth perception or misjudging distances influence one's interpersonal relations? How does difficulty with visual/auditory perceptual input, integration of what one perceives, memory storage and retrieval or language/motor output influence nonacademic learning and functioning? Selective perception, association, processing and communication difficulties do indeed influence social as well as academic learning.

SOCIAL SKILLS AND ACADEMIC SUCCESS

Numerous investigations in the 1970s indicate that adequate social skills are essential to academic success. See, for example, Cartledge and Milburn's review (1978). Problems related to social and emotional development should be a focus of direct instruction and complement academic instruction emphasizing changing inappropriate behaviors. Emotional well-being and favorable attitudes and peer interactions facilitate effective academic learning.

Bryan and Bryan (1978) reviewed research on social behavior and found LD children likely to be rejected by peers, parents and teachers, and to have poor perception of subtle social cues. Thus most LD children need specific and conscious training to develop social skills. In an article on intervention, LeGreca and Mesibov (1979) suggested nine areas of training including smiling and laughing with peers, greeting others, joining ongoing activities, conversing, sharing and cooperating, and grooming and physical appearance.

Social skills enumeration and training programs vary widely and are age-related. ASSET, an example of a program for junior high students, includes a film series and work materials. It involves skills such as giving positive feedback, giving/accepting negative feedback, resolving conflicts with people and problem solving. The skill development on resisting peer pressure, to give one example, includes practicing a serious and concerned way of approaching a person, saying something positive to the person ("You are a good friend . . ." or "I like you . . .") and firmly stating what you'll resist (". . . but I'm not going to . . ."). Other steps include giving a personal reason for not doing something ("I can't afford to get into trouble . . ."). If peer pressure continues, repeat that you will not do it and leave the situation ("No, I'm not going to . . . I'll see you . . .").

We should teach children to conceptualize their behaviors and how they contribute to outcomes such as peer rejection; what occurred before, during and after an event, and how did behavior(s) cause rejection? Training should give children "response banks" from which they can draw behaviors as needed. Here is an example of a direct request: "Please let me finish my sentences. I talk slowly but I can tell you things better when you let me finish." Turn apologies into compliments: "Thank you for being patient with me." (That can replace "I'm sorry I made you drop your books.") It is important to practice behaviors until they can be used spontaneously.

Mercer (1979) suggested use of the Extreme Game with LD children and some friends to help those with poor self-management skills (self-control, self-help, independent problem solving, etc.). Describe a real-life incident and have them, especially the target children, tell the worst thing one could have done and discuss best alternatives.

There are many helpful ideas for improving social skills. Knonick (1981, p. 182) suggested that a role playing session structured by a teacher may be made a learning experience by including in the process "cues for attention, modeling, positive reinforcement, small increments in difficulty, and opportunity for overlearning." Role playing can be used with older children or adolescents for teaching interpersonal problem solving involving genuine behavior problems in groups using the technique. Examples include handling teasing or anger, dealing with rules and authority, and requesting help.

Problem solving skills should include attention to cause-effect dynamics, anticipating consequences of some specific behaviors, understanding some alternative solutions to situations and goal planning.

STRATEGIES FROM VARYING PERSPECTIVES

Effectiveness of a variety of strategies for changing social and emotional problem behaviors from various theoretical perspectives gives support to the likelihood that many of them result from a variety of causes. Ecological strategies include behaviors and reactions to them by others in the ecosystem. In settings such as special education classes or summer camps programs can emphasize cooperative efforts between children and others who interact with them. Physiological or biological treatment may include psychostimulants, megavitamins and/or dietary regulation with some emphasis on structured environment for such behaviors as poor attention and hyperactivity. Psychodynamic programs include therapeutic counseling and family dynamics and deal with negative feelings and self-concept, and with gaining insight and desire to change to more positive actions. Behavior management and modification procedures include systematic use of rewards and punishers, contingency contracting, counterconditioning and engineered classrooms.

SOME CHANGE TECHNIQUES

In addition to social skills training discussed above, some useful techniques for developing positive behaviors and feelings include life space interviewing (LSI), participant modeling and mutual story telling.

LSI is a process of discussing in depth a behavioral situation to aid a child in understanding self, gaining insight into problem behaviors, and developing a solution or an action plan in which support is given by the teacher(s) and/or others. The interviewing by a person significant to the child should be done soon after a crisis or behavioral occurrence. Teachers and counselors can learn effective interviewing skills and empathy to use this technique by studying available materials (Morse 1971; Heuchert 1983) and by practicing and criticizing each other's LSIs. Combining other techniques such as puppetry and role playing with LSI may be useful in helping LD children.

Participant modeling can be used by parents, teachers or others modeling problem solving behavior with self-verbalizing solutions (such as staying on task, interacting with peers or working math problems). Then children model working through similar problems while self-verbalizing, with adult feedback as needed to correct or expand their solutions. Half-hour modeling sessions on three or four occasions generally yield noticeable results. Millman et al. (1980) would describe a child's self-verbalizing like this in response to modeling listening and executing instructions to copy a picture: "What does the teacher want me to do? I'm suppose to copy the picture (self-instruction). First I draw a line (self-reinforcement). I did that one well. Now I draw this part . . ." And so it goes. Modeling can help a child learn cognitive control. It has been suggested that in modeling an adult should sometimes make an error on purpose and then correct it immediately to illustrate that process.

Mutual story telling was developed as a therapeutic technique by Richard Gardner (1971) whose training workshops attract school psychologists, counselors, social workers and other professionals. A child is asked to make up a story for a radio or television program and tell it on cassette tape. The story is analyzed and the therapist tells a story using the same characters and settings but portraying healthier and more appropriate solutions to major conflicts or decisions. Gardner's goal in working with LD children is to treat secondary emotional problems such as anxiety, anger, low self-concept, family conflicts, etc. This technique involves modeling and positive reinforcement along with overlearning by tape-recorded playback.

SOCIAL DEVELOPMENT

Let's look at a couple of specific problems in social development which occur within an interpersonal context and which relate to responding to others.

Disruptiveness may be caused by inappropriate social learning or by attention-seeking, inability to work independently, boredom, lack of interest in tasks or other reasons. Some LD children bother, disturb, distract or in some way disrupt others — even entire classes. Some of these youngsters are the picky-pokey kind; they trip, punch, or pick at someone, or they poke, hit, throw objects, or engage in some type of physical contact which disturbs classmates. Others make faces, clown, name-call or talk or laugh at inappropriate times. Some engage in physical and non-physical disruptions so frequently that it's difficult to find non-disrupting behaviors for which to reward them. Sometimes keeping a small chart on a child's or teacher's desk or a home desk, for recording each disruption will help reduce the number. Who wants a behavior record kept by the teacher/ parent? Asking the child to report disruptive behavior in class to parents, and planning for feedback to be sure he did, helps some children reduce disruptiveness. Making the disruptive behavior unpleasant by asking the child to practice it during recess or when other children have free time can reduce its occurrence in the future. Algozzine (1982) has made additional suggestions for changing non-attentive and irrelevant behaviors.

Social withdrawal, isolation, or shyness interfere with meaningful interpersonal relationships and with learning self-expression. Structuring some

activities so the withdrawn child is expected to interact in ways in which
you are relatively certain he can be successful is a useful approach to change.
Pairing children can often increase interaction as can rewarding volunteer-
ing answers or comments during class discussion. Obviously, it is important to avoid embarrassing a withdrawn child when he does interact. Give
such a child an important task or responsibility at times when other children will want to interact with him.

EMOTIONAL DEVELOPMENT

While it is difficult to separate emotional from social behaviors, in this
presentation emotional problems are regarded as unproductive intrain-
dividual responses to need gratification or situations which need solutions.
Consideration of possible reasons for a behavior can aid us in assisting
a child in changing it. To what extent is emotional development effected
by neurological dysfunctioning? Some recent research points toward the
front of the brain cortex being more involved with emotional functions
than the back with the possibility that happy feelings are controlled by
the left and sad feelings by the right frontal side.

Self-esteem or self-concept is formed from feedback a child gets from
others. When a child's actions or statements about his abilities prevent him
from responding to previous learning or attempting new exercises, we infer that he has poor or negative self-esteem. Statements reflecting antici-
pated or actual failure due to perceived inadequacies are familiar to us —
"That's too hard!" "I can't do it!" What do you think I am, a walking book?"
Praising a child for what he does well, asking him to be a peer tutor involving tasks he can do, allowing him to choose activities in which he can
succeed, helping him with grooming and physical appearance, displaying
his best work, and asking him to tell his parents about progress are a few
things we can do to help a child increase his self-worth or self-esteem.

Many LD children have low frustration tolerance or low level of with-
standing frustration which interferes with productive efforts. Rewarding
progress toward a goal, helping a child pace himself to reduce frustration,
giving alternative tasks or amounts of work which he can complete, help
develop coping skills and increase tolerance level.

Intense anxiety, uneasiness, or apprehension may interfere significantly
with learning and functioning, while mild anxiety can be constructive in
motivating learning or avoidance of dangers. Possible early sources of strong
anxiety are insecurity, excessive frustration and inconsistent parental behaviors and standards coupled with negative evaluations of a child's behavior. Overhearing adult talk about problems which a child sees as un-

solvable is another source of anxiety. Numerous physical reactions are associated with anxiety — e.g., nausea, tense muscles or increased activity. Fortunately, anxiety is responsive to a large number of techniques such as psychodrama and role playing in which a child can act out feelings and some solutions. Experiences which increase a child's successes, self-confidence and assertiveness can help reduce anxiety.

While depression doesn't seem to be one of the most frequent emotional problems of LD children, we should consider it because of its danger and the possibility of its occurrence among those with poor self-esteem. Some of its major components are feelings of guilt, helplessness, loss, or grief. It may be expressed not only in feelings of sadness but in disruptiveness, acting out, psychosomatic ailments, aggressiveness, and even in lethargy. Acute or short-term depression often has an identifiable cause such as the loss of a parent or other loved one, or thing such as a pet, or withdrawal of affection. Supportive counseling can help a child express feelings of loss or rejection so he can deal with them. Long-term or chronic depression is more severe and may involve suicide threats or attempts and deep feelings of worthlessness and helplessness. Chronic depression generally requires long-term therapy and frequently involves need for anti-depressant medication. School psychologists should be involved in treating depressed children and can provide consultation to assist teachers and parents in helping children confront painful feelings and express feelings of helplessness and worthlessness so they can be modified by re-evaluation of personal attributes and other measures which enhance self-esteem and confidence. Referral to other community agencies which can work with the family involved is often appropriate.

Emotional and social development and behavior of gifted LD children is a whole area which needs continued and expanded research.

IMMATURE BEHAVIORS

Behaviors such as hyperactivity, distractibility, impulsiveness, messiness and sloppiness, procrastination and dawdling, daydreaming and poor coordination are called immature behaviors by Millman, Schaefer and Cohen (1980, p. 120) who stated that "most evidence points to a central nervous system dysfunction as the cause of these inhibitory control problems" and that there may be a brain structure development lag which causes some forms of behavioral immaturity. The behaviors discussed here are immature when they are inappropriate for the child's age or similar to behavior of younger children. Millman and his colleagues consider methods most frequently used to promote maturation or more age-appropriate behaviors to include training in specific skills, modeling, positive reinforcement and especially praise, contracting and points systems as a way of earning privileges, and positive self-verbalizations by children.

Modeling and self-verbalization are recommended for reducing hyperactivity. Behavioral management may include daily reports and individually selected rewards to reduce hyperactivity. Some other suggestions worth trying include: use of background music, allowing short intervals of activities so children don't have to sit for three consecutive periods, and physical education programs.

Most children by the time they are ten years old understand the concept of time and have the maturity to plan time and be punctual, while those under six need to have time and situations structured for them. Some people use the term task-avoidance to describe activities involving fruitless use of time—staring at the book, flipping pages, sharpening pencils needlessly, e.g.—and others call them dawdling. Procrastination is the putting off of things that should be done in intentional and habitual ways. Whether you call it task-avoidance, procrastination, or dawdling, the result is frequent tardiness for events or lateness in handing in work. Methods of change focus on trying to get children to decrease the time needed and to be accurate in their work by rewarding them with privileges when they do so.

Counter-productive behaviors which result in task-interference are signs of immature behavior. Which behaviors would you enumerate? Robby, for example, roams around the room and walks to the window and stares out; Sally plays with materials and toys she brings from home even after dozens of reminders not to do so or she goes to the bathroom and runs the lavatory water. What can you do to change these interferring behaviors? One suggestion is that you work out an agreement/contract about the number of times one needs to sharpen pencils or go to the bathroom and give the child that number of "passes"; in an effort to gradually reduce the number of interferences, you can gradually reduce the number of "passes."

Writing the words "be neater" across a paper will not change Kathy's untidy work. Perhaps Millman and colleagues are correct; extremely messy and sloppy behavior is a immature approach. To change this central nervous system functioning/dysfunctioning, persistence will be needed. Try having a child practice organizing his things or specific kinds of work; give positive reinforcement for neatness and organization.

Daydreaming or being apparently "lost in thought" or "living in one's own world" may be due to deep emotional problems or preoccupations or due to not having learned to hold one's attention or focus on tasks. We all occasionally fantasize or imagine about things which are unattainable in real life and that is healthy at appropriate times and when done only occasionally. What's harmful about Fulton daydreaming or "living in his own world?" You know—his attention is not on those instructions you're giving him or on the assignments/tasks he is suppose to be completing like most of the others are doing. Recently I observed some sixth grade students in a small language arts class being taught by an outstanding "regular" teacher. When Charley (not his real name) kept looking into space and not getting his seatwork done, she walked by his desk and quietly put her hand on the paper he was supposed to be completing and he resumed his work. A few minutes later, he showed signs of preoccupation with something other than completing his paper for about 60 seconds and that time she walked near him and motioned toward the work which he resumed again. Her simple and inconspicuous ways of calling his attention back to his work were effective and easily done. An additional way of helping Charley stay on-task to get that seatwork done would be to give him points to reward attentiveness to his work which would be in some way a way of giving him positive reinforcement. Many children and youth find the choosing of an activity of interest to them very reinforcing. The activity of interest can be one which is also a learning or practicing of learning so it is really not a waste of time if the activities from which they select are worthwhile ones.

Now let's consider impulsivity—acting without prior thinking or without considering possible consequences—such as writing or marking or blurting out orally the very first response that occurs to a child. Impulsivity seems to be a characteristic behavior of a very large proportion of LD children. Our goal is to change the impulsive non-reflective tempo to a reflective cognitive one, to develop a more deliberate approach and a more accurate response set. Impulsivity is associated not only with poor school achievement but with social difficulties of many kinds. When Joey blurts out a sassy comment when he has been sent to the principal or says an inappropriate comment to a bully or to a timid girl, it gets him into social difficulties. Think about how it effects sibling and parental relationships! Some methods currently used to develop impulse control include these: modeling, self-reinforcement, self-verbalizing ("stop," "look," "listen" and "think about it first"), use of oral or printed reminders, encouraging delayed responding and fantasy training. An article in *Journal of Abnormal Child Psychology* (Cullinan, Epstein, and Silver 1977) gives good suggestions for modifying impulsive tempo.

OTHER NEEDS

LD children have more social skills and socio-emotional needs than can be addressed in a single presentation. We should at least cite the need for improved body awareness, the need to improve perception of proper location and positioning in relation to the environment. Poor coordination and poor spatial relations contribute to the need for improved body awareness and relationships. We need to help some LD children learn appropriate times to laugh and appropriate facial expressions. The need to learn constructive expression of both negative and positive feelings is important for social and emotional health and can be met by several of the methods described previously including modeling and role playing, methods which are usually enjoyable to people of all ages.

FAMILY DYNAMICS

The role of the family is crucial, of course, in a child's development. The family may add to or provide support for socio-emotional stresses. Parents and siblings, as well as the LD child, need help in understanding the disability and their reactions to it and in examining family dynamics to see how they may help alleviate rather than exaggerate problems. Kronick's study, *Three Families* (1976), reports vivid reminders of the importance of organization of time, space, and mechanics of living, use of language, expression of anger, etc. The book should be read by all parents of LD children, school personnel including teachers, and other professionals who serve the learning disabled.

Our efforts to help the LD child need to encompass the *total* child, not just his writing or reading or other area of achievement deficit, and to involve his total ecology. When the school environment and the home environment and dynamics are coordinated more successes will occur. PL 94-142's focus on providing an appropriate education must be complemented by many other public and private services such as family education and counseling, if the whole child is to get maximum support in his total environment. ACLD chapters are important and vital forces in family education and support.

BECOMING ADVOCATES

Prerequisite to remedial and compensatory instruction involving academic and social and emotional components, is the child's own recognition and understanding *at his level* of his learning differences. While other professionals and parents have responsibilities, it is this presenter's judgment that the school psychologist has a key and unique role in providing information which can be used by the child in moving toward understanding his learning strengths and weaknesses so that he will not feel guilty or ashamed and so that as he progresses through his educational course he can become his own advocate. Involving individual children in their IEP development is worth the effort it takes.

CONCLUSION

Beliefs of parents, teachers and other professionals about themselves and other persons sometime "rub off" or are indirectly learned by the young. Even when they are not learned unconsciously by many LD children, they do influence what we decide is worth doing through direct and carefully designed programs and influence the selection of methods and techniques. They also influence our setting of priorities so that socioemotional development and social skills are included in our services along with our emphasis on the cognitive aspects of learning. Because we value them, we show respect for, interest in, helpfulness to, concern for, and discipline of LD children in order to maximize their social, emotional and intellectual development.

REFERENCES

Algozzine, B. *Problem Behavior Management: Educator's Resource Service.* Rockville, Md.: Aspen, 1982.

Association for Children and Adults with Learning Disabilities. "The Link between Learning Disabilities and Juvenile Delinquency." *ACLD Newsbriefs* (March–April 1982).

Bryan, T., and J. Bryan. *Understanding Learning Disabilities,* 2nd ed. Port Washington, N.Y.: Alfred, 1978.

Cartledge, G., and J. F. Milburn, eds. *Teaching Social Skills to Children: Innovative Approaches.* Elmsford, N.Y.: Pergamon Press, 1980.

_____. "The Case for Teaching Social Skills in the Classroom: A Review." *Review of Educational Research,* 481 (1978): 133–156.

Cullinan, C., M. H. Epstein, and L. Silver. "Modification of Impulsive Tempo in LD Pupils." *Journal of Abnormal Child Psychology,* 5 (1977): 437–444.

Gardner, R. A. *Therapeutic Communication with Children: The Mutual Story-Telling Technique.* New York: Science House, 1971.

Heuchert, C. M. "Can Teachers Change Behavior? Try Interviews!" *Academic Therapy* 18, no. 3 (1983): 321–328.

Johnson D., and H. Myklebust. *Learning Disabilities: Educational Principles and Practices.* New York: Grune and Stratton, 1967.

Kronick, D. *Social Development of Learning Disabled Persons.* San Francisco: Jossey-Bass, 1981.

————. *Three Families: The Effect of Family Dynamics in Social and Conceptual Learning.* Novato, Cal.: Academic Therapy, 1976.

LeGreca, A. M., and G. B. Mesibov. "Social Skills Intervention with Learning Disabled Children." *Clinical Child Psychology* 8 (1979): 234–241.

Lerner, J. W. *Learning Disabilities,* 3rd ed. Boston: Houghton-Mifflin, 1981.

Mercer, C. D. *Children and Adolescents with Learning Disabilities.* Columbus: Merrill, 1979.

Millman, H. L., C. E. Schaefer, and J. J. Cohen. *Therapies for School Behavior Problems.* San Francisco: Jossey-Bass, 1980.

Morse, W. C. "Worksheet on Life Space Interviewing for Teachers." In N. J. Long, W. C. Morse, and R. G. Newman, eds. *Conflict in the Classroom.* Belmont, Cal.: Wadsworth, 1971.

O'Leary, K., and S. O'Leary. *Classroom Management: The Successful Use of Behavior Modification.* New York: Pergamon Press, 1977.

Omizo, M. M., S. H. Redner, and R. H. McPherson. "Modeling: An Effective Teaching Strategy." *Academic Therapy* 18, no. 3 (1983) 365–368.

Research Press. *ASSET: A Social Skills Program for Adolescents.* Champaign, Ill.: Research Press, 1982.

Rotatori, A. F., and A. J. Mauser. "IEP Assessment for LD Students." *Academic Therapy* 16, no. 2 (1980): 141–153.

Silver, L. B. "Frequency of Adoption of Children with Neurological LD Syndrome." *Journal of Learning Disabilities* 3 (1970): 307–310.

EDUCATIONAL AND
SOCIAL TECHNIQUES

5

Coping Means Survival
for Learning Disabled Adolescents

Elaine Fine and Shirley Zeitlin

LEARNING DISABLED ADOLESCENTS often have maladaptive coping behaviors that were learned to protect them from the stress of their failure. It is these behaviors, though not tied to intellectual capabilities (Yeargan 1982), that become more debilitating than academic deficiencies as the individual enters late adolescence and young adulthood (Kronick 1978; Werner and Smith 1982). To help them survive, they need to learn more adaptive coping strategies.

The characteristics manifested by many learning disabled adolescents that preclude their development of adaptive coping strategies include lack of organizational skills, passivity in learning situations, excessive reliance on external cues for feedback, lack of flexibility, inability to generalize, difficulties in sustaining attention, poor tolerance for frustration, and inadequate social skills.

The school is one place where these strategies can be learned. Teaching them is a two-step process: identification of the student's coping resources (or lack of them) and adaptation of the curriculum to include opportunities for the student to learn the strategies needed to cope more adaptively.

This chapter addresses the two steps. The Coping Inventory, an instrument used to assess the behaviors most related to adaptive coping, is described. Case studies of two learning disabled adolescent students are given to demonstrate how the results of the Coping Inventory are used to develop plans to teach coping strategies within the framework of an existing curriculum.

The Coping Inventory (Zeitlin 1982) is a criterion referenced instrument developed from the results of Murphy's eighteen-year longitudinal study of children's coping behavior (Murphy and Moriarty 1976).

The word *coping* is used as a general term for one type of adaptive behavior that describes *the behaviors a person uses to meet his own needs and to adapt to the demands of his environment.* It is an active, adaptive process learned from the interactions of many different facets; the person's developmental pattern, temperament, prior experience, general level of competence, personal value system, areas of vulnerability and the demands of the environment. Coping effectiveness ranges on a continuum from being adaptive to being maladaptive.

Factor analysis of the observational data of Murphy's study identified two major categories: coping with the environment and coping with self. Coping with the environment is defined as "the capacity to cope with the opportunities, challenges, frustrations, and threats in the environment." In other words, it is how the child adapts to his environment. Coping with self is "the capacity to manage one's relation to the environment so as to maintain integrated functioning (this contrasted with vulnerability)." It is how the child meets his own survival and growth needs.

The Coping Inventory is divided into these two categories — Self and Environment — and three bipolar dimensions used to describe coping style: non-productive-productive, passive-active, and rigid-flexible. A total of 48 items are observed and rated on a scale of 1 (least adaptive) to 5 (most adaptive). *Adaptive coping* is behavior that enhances efforts to care for oneself and/or responds appropriately to the demands of the environment. When the person copes adaptively, he is open to new experiences. *Maladaptive coping* is behavior that defeats efforts to care for oneself and/or responds inappropriately to the demands of the environment. The behavior may appear to help the person manage the stress at the moment. Maladaptive coping interferes with new learning because the person uses his efforts to protect himself from failure. As a result, vulnerability is increased and excessive stress may be generated over time.

The concept of coping focuses on what the person is trying to do and the personal resources available to do it. It, in itself, does not imply success, but effort. Coping is a process; adaptation is a result; mastery is an achievement.

ASSUMPTIONS

Some of the assumptions on which the Coping Inventory is based on are:

1. Coping is predominately a single factor concept. Categories and dimensions used in the Coping Inventory are descriptive. A change in any one behavior will have an impact on the total field.
2. The formal characteristics of coping behaviors are the same for all individuals regardless of age, sex, culture or intelligence. The specific actions by which the behavior is implemented vary.
3. Clusters of behavior in the Coping Inventory relate to specific variables (i.e. intelligence, self concept, language, temperament, social competence)

and therefore may have some interrelation, but coping (as the integrated behavior) is more comprehensive and complex than any individual dimension.

4. Coping behaviors are learned; therefore, they can be acquired, changed or eliminated.
5. There are many different strategies that can be used to effectively change coping behavior.

The Coping Inventory has two forms; one for observation and one for self-rating. Both are appropriate for adolescents and sometimes it is useful to use both to identify differences in perceptions of effectiveness. These differences can be used as the basis of discussion or counseling.

The Coping Inventory is scored to yield an Adaptive Behavior Index (ABI) which is the average of all scores and is converted to the same numerical scale of 1 to 5 used for the initial rating and has the same values. There are separate scores for each category (self-environment) and each dimension (Productive-Active and Flexible). Most and least adaptive behaviors are listed. A graphic profile of the results is also used as an aid in interpretation.

Technical data pertaining to validity and reliability of the instrument is published in its manual (Zeitlin 1980).

The Coping Inventory results of Richard and Debbie are presented to demonstrate how they are used to develop strategies. An ecological model, basic to the concept of assessment of coping, is also used for initial planning. In an ecological model, assessment is geared to an analysis of the person that takes into account the many environments in which the person operates, as well as the person's interactions in these environments. In planning for instruction, the same parameters are considered.

STRATEGY DEVELOPMENT

Each strategy that is developed for adolescents must be consistent with the major developmental tasks of that age which include a need for self-esteem, the earned esteem of peers, self-confidence, and growth towards independence. It also must consider the impact of the learning disability on the achievement of tasks. The selection of strategies should be relevant to the demands placed on the adolescent; in school, the goal for most learning disabled adolescents is to either get the student ready to be mainstreamed or to help ensure that the mainstreaming experience is successful. Therefore, the strategies developed need to facilitate self-control since the mainstreamed student must assume responsibility for his or her own actions and decrease the dependence previously fostered in special education classrooms. The strategies also must enhance peer interaction which is a necessity for successful mainstreaming.

Strategy development to increase adaptive behavior for the learning disabled should follow general effective principles for instructing the learning disabled. Strengths, or most adaptive behaviors, of the student should be capitalized on in order to further enhance them so that they can compensate for deficiencies. Direct instruction in areas of weakness, or least adaptive behaviors, should be provided in small steps with sufficient practice and reinforcement on each step and attention given to generalization from the controlled teaching situation to new, real-life situations. Consistent feedback provided to the adolescent and provisions for self-monitoring are needed to make the strategies truly efficient and lasting. Adolescents with a learning disability should not be overwhelmed with too many strategies at once since their effectiveness is decreased when under stress and when they feel overwhelmed. They should participate in deciding which behaviors are priorities for change. While many of the strategies can be taught to groups of students and are useful for increasing different types of adaptive behavior, strategy development should be individualized. Strategy development can be facilitated by a resource room teacher, as a regular part of the instruction for the learning disabled adolescent, or by a counselor.

CASE STUDIES: RICHARD

Richard is a 14-year-old boy with a learning disability who is classified as neurologically impaired. He is placed in a special class and participates in a pre-vocational program. Richard's Adaptive Behavior Summary showing his Coping Inventory scores are in Figure 5.1. He has an ABI of 2.1 which indicates, on the whole, that he has minimally effective coping behaviors. His highest score (2.7) is in the self-active dimension which indicates that he is most effective in actively trying to meet his own needs. His lowest scores are in the self-flexible dimensions, indicating that his rigid behaviors interfere most with his ability to cope adaptively.

Richard has 11 items (of 48) rated 1 (behavior is not effective). Of these 11, 8 are in the 2 flexible-rigid dimensions and 3 in environment active. Based on the assumption that a change in any single behavior will influence total functioning, the least effective behavior in the least effective dimension is used to develop strategies for intervention. Because Rich-

Figure 5.1. Richard's Adaptive Behavior Summary.

C.A. - 14 years

COPING - SELF				COPING - ENVIRONMENT		
	Raw Score	Converted Score			Raw Score	Converted Score
PRODUCTIVE	28	2.3		PRODUCTIVE	25	2.1
ACTIVE	16	2.7		ACTIVE	11	1.8
FLEXIBLE	10	1.7		FLEXIBLE	11	1.8
		TOTAL 6.65			TOTAL	5.74
	SELF SCORE 2.2			ENVIRONMENT SCORE 1.9		

Sum of SELF SCORE and ENVIRONMENT SCORE   4.13

Key Self _____
     Env. _ _ _ _   ADAPTIVE BEHAVIOR INDEX   2.1

COPING PROFILE

	1	2	3	4	5	
Non-Productive						Productive
Passive						Active
Rigid						Flexible

MOST ADAPTIVE BEHAVIORS				LEAST ADAPTIVE BEHAVIORS			
Cat.	Dim.	Rat.		Cat.	Dim.	Rat.	
S	A	4	Reacts to sensory stimulation.	S	F	1	Doesn't shift plans or change behavior.
S	P	4	Responds to external controls.	S	F	1	Cannot accept substitute.
				S	F	1	Cannot manage stress.
S	P	3	Uses language to express needs.	S	F	1	Not independent or self reliant.
E	P	3	Understands directions.	S	F	1	Isn't creative and original.

ard's scores in Environment Flexible and Active are almost as low (1.8), intervention could also have been started there. A decision is made to select no more than 5 or 6 behaviors, because efforts to change too many behaviors at one time usually prove frustrating and ineffective.

Richard has no items that are rated 5 (effective more of the time). He has two items rated 4 (effective more often than not) and two items rated 3 (effective in some situations, but not others). These four are listed as his most adaptive behaviors and are used to help plan the most successful strategies.

In designing an individualized plan to teach Richard strategies that would enhance his coping ability, his relative strength in responding to external controls was built on; it was decided to attempt to assist Richard in internalizing controls so that he can become more independent rather than continuing his dependence on others to provide controls. An intermediate step which included having Richard use routine recording of specific behaviors was designed utilizing one of his least adaptive behaviors, an inability to monitor his energy level. He was trained to chart his activity level at set intervals and reviewed this with the facilitator. This self-monitoring process itself has helped the individual to change the behavior being recorded in a positive direction (Loper 1982). Thus, this strategy capitalizes on a strength to strengthen a less adaptive behavior and helps Richard move toward placing his actions more directly under his control.

A second strategy for Richard also utilized a strength, his ability to use language to express needs and was based on work from the field of cognitive behavior modification which seeks to train deficient learners to use cognitive strategies that highly successful learners use to approach a wide variety of problems. One strategy, based on the model of Meichenbaum (Meichenbaum and Goodman 1971) is the use of self-verbalization which involves teaching Richard specific verbalizations that follow a step-by-step sequence. This strategy addressed an academic deficiency in Richard's Individualized Educational Program, an inability to complete mathematical word problems. After learning a systematic strategy for doing the word problems, self-verbalization was taught using the steps of modeling by the facilitator aloud while he observed, having him rehearse with assistance and then alone, having him perform the task with whispered self-verbalizations, and then using silent verbalizations. The four types of self-verbalizations that were designed for Richard to help him do the word problems were problem definition, focusing of attention, coping statements, and self-reinforcement. This strategy enabled Richard to meet an academic demand and gave him the tool to increase independent functioning because learning is put under his own control. Richard's independence and self-reliance will be developed.

Richard's least adaptive behaviors include an inability to manage stress and a difficulty in shifting plans and changing behavior. Direct instruction was provided in the area using a model developed by Fagen, Long, and Stevens (1975) in which Richard, in a group setting, is taught to understand and accept frustration through a controlled frustration experience induced by the facilitator and followed by a directed discussion. The model also includes training in coping with frustration by learning effective methods such as modifying the goal, seeking help, or letting go of the goal. The training should assist Richard in developing a wider repertoire of behaviors to cope with frustration.

In summary, in interpreting Richard's Coping Inventory, decisions needed to be made as to which strategies were priority behaviors for change and which few strategies would be most facilitative for that change. For Richard the decision was to train him to use self-monitoring techniques, self-verbalization, and direct instruction in coping with frustration.

CASE STUDIES: DEBBIE

Debbie is a 15-year-old girl with a learning disability who is classified as perceptually impaired. She receives instruction in a resource room for reading and science and has recently been mainstreamed for her other subjects. Debbie's Adaptive Behavior Summary showing her Coping Inventory scores are in Figure 5.2. She has an ABI of 2.7 which indicates that she is effective in some situations, but not in others. Her highest scores (3.0) are in the environment-active and the self-productive dimensions indicating that she is most effective in actively making efforts to cope with her environment and to productively meet her own needs. Her lowest score is in the environment-productive dimension which indicates difficulty in using socially responsible behaviors that produce desired effects.

Debbie, like Richard, had 11 items rated 1 (behavior is not effective). Of these 6 are clustered in the environment-productive dimension, which indicates that she demonstrates non-productive behavior in coping with the environment; this area is associated with difficulty in social skills. Two of Debbie's 1 ratings were in the self-active dimension and indicate that she has difficulty using appropriate verbal and non-verbal communications to get her needs met. These become the basis for planning for change.

Debbie has two items that are rated 5 (effective most of the time and thirteen items rated 4 (effective more often than not). These indicate strength in handling frustration, staying with a task, using appropriate impulse control, having a high energy level, and enjoying new situations. She has many personal resources but cannot translate them to use when interacting with others.

The first strategy was developed to help Debbie in making her needs known and to help her become actively involved in situations. Failure to

Figure 5.2. Debbie's Adaptive Behavior Summary.

C.A.:   15 years

COPING-SELF	Raw Score	Converted Score		COPING – ENVIRONMENT	Raw Score	Converted Score
PRODUCTIVE	36	3.0	PRODUCTIVE	21		2.1
ACTIVE	15	2.5	ACTIVE	15		3.0
FLEXIBLE	16	2.7	FLEXIBLE	13		2.7
		TOTAL 8.2			TOTAL	7.8
	SELF SCORE 2.7			ENVIRONMENT SCORE	2.6	

Sum of SELF SCORE and ENVIRONMENT SCORE   5.3

Key: Self _____
Env. _ _ _ _

ADAPTIVE BEHAVIOR INDEX   2.7

COPING PROFILE

	1	2	3	4	5	
Non-Productive						Productive
Passive						Active
Rigid						Flexible

MOST ADAPTIVE BEHAVIORS

Cat.	Dim.	Rat.	
S	A	5	Accepts substitutes when necessary.
E	P	5	Understands and responds to directions without external help.
S	P	4	Four dimensions were rated here and deal with handling frustration and anxiety well.
S	A	4	Stays with task and has effective impulse control- 2 items
E	P	4	Is curious.
E	A	4	Five items were rated here and deal with having a good energy level, enjoying newness.

LEAST ADAPTIVE BEHAVIORS

Cat.	Dim.	Rat.	
S	A	1	Cannot communicate to others disagreement or feelings, verbally or non-verbally.
S	A	1	Cannot initiate action to get needs met.
S	F	1	Cannot balance independence with sufficient dependence to be able to get and use help
E	P	1	Six items were rated here and deal with difficulties in social skills, reacting appropriately to others, and understanding the implications of her behavior.
E	A	1	Does not actively involve self

do this has made her excessively dependent on others and, while it may be appropriate for a younger learning disabled person to rely on others to intervene, explain, and obtain help, adolescents need to begin to develop independence by relying on their own resources to meet their needs.

Debbie, therefore, was trained to be an advocate for herself through role-playing and videotaping real-life situations in school in which she had to make her needs known in order to obtain services. For example, due to her reading problem, she has difficulty reading aloud. She feared asking to be excused from reading aloud in her English class because she did not want to be different and felt the teacher would judge her as stupid. The facilitator, who in this case was the resource room teacher, could have made the arrangement with the English teacher, but this would have again made Debbie dependent on others rather than fostering independence. A prerequisite to training Debbie in self-advocacy was to ensure that she understood her learning disability and the effect it has on her functioning. After Debbie practiced self-advocacy with her resource teacher, she was asked to meet with the English teacher. At the first meeting, the resource teacher accompanied her but took a back-seat role, being available in case there were unforeseen difficulties and cueing Debbie as she went through the meeting. Having the resource teacher present gave Debbie support and also allowed the opportunity for Debbie to receive feedback after the meeting so that she could refine her newly acquired skill. Debbie's strengths in dealing with frustration and handling situations with energy and appropriate controls allowed her to participate in this new training so that she could learn to capitalize on her personal resources when interacting with others.

Debbie's deficiencies in social skills prevent her from interacting with peers and adults. Social misperception prevents her from reacting appropriately to verbal and non-verbal behavior of others and from understanding the implications of her behavior. Direct instruction in social skills was undertaken using real-life experiences employing many practice techniques, and incorporating principles for effective instruction for learning disabled persons. Guidelines for instruction in social development outlined by Kronick (1981) were followed.

In summary, in interpreting Debbie's Coping Inventory, decisions were made regarding priority behaviors. Self-advocacy and social skills training were selected as the strategies which would be most productive in enabling Debbie to use her many personal resources in interacting with others and getting her needs met, two essentials for successful mainstreaming.

The strategies designed for these two adolescents were based on individual needs as assessed with the Coping Inventory and will increase their repertoire of adaptive behaviors; this will lead to redirecting behavioral patterns which often cause the learning disabled adolescent to be isolated from activities that would contribute to adult functioning. The new strategies can, with practice, be generalized to many situations and will enable the individuals to more successfully compensate for their learning disabilities and meet the developmental tasks of adolescence. Developing individualized plans for increasing adaptive behavior as part of the planning done for learning disabled students in schools will help these adolescents to actualize their potential so that the learning disability does not handicap their ability to cope.

REFERENCES

Fagen, S., N. Long, and D. Stevens. *Teaching Children Self-Control.* Columbus, Ohio: Charles Merrill, 1975.

Kronick, D. "An Examination of Psychosocial Aspects of Learning Disabled Adolescents." *Learning Disability Quarterly,* (1978): 86–93.

_____. *Social Development of Learning Disabled Persons.* San Francisco: Jossey-Bass, 1981.

Loper, A. B. "Metacognitive Training to Correct Academic Deficiency." *Topics in Learning and Learning Disabilities* (1982): 61–68.

Meichenbaum, D. H., and J. Goodman. "Teaching Impulsive Children to Talk to Themselves: A Means of Developing Self-Control." *Journal of Abnormal Psychology* (1971): 115–126.

Murphy, L., and A. Moriarty. *Vulnerability, Coping, and Growth.* New Haven, Ct.: Yale University Press, 1976.

Wernel, E., and R. Smith. *Vulnerable but Invincible: A Longitudinal Study of Resilient Children and Youth.* New York: McGraw-Hill, 1982.

Yeargen, D. R. A factor-analytic study of adaptive behavior and intellectual functioning in learning disabled children.

Zeitlin, S. *Manual for the Coping Inventory* (Rev. ed.). Upper Montclair, N.J.: Innovative Educational Materials, 1980.

_____. *The Coping Inventory.* Upper Montclair, N.J.: Innovative Educational Materials, 1982.

6

The Application of Study Techniques with Learning Disabled Adolescents

Linda Mixon Clary

ADOLESCENT LEARNING DISABLED STUDENTS at the middle school, secondary, and college levels have been described by a variety of characteristics that include the following (Kronick 1982):

1. disorganized in planning how to use time and complete tasks
2. limited in the ability to look at problems, analyse them, and select reasonable alternatives
3. rigid in their habits
4. disorganized in scheduling time to the point of being unproductive
5. egocentric in judgment which limits their being able to visualize another individual's perspective and the learner's relationship to that perspective
6. unrealistic in setting goals that result in expecting too much or too little

All of these factors, obviously, make it very difficult for LD adolescents to do what is demanded most of them—study and learn independently.

Adolescence itself compounds the problems of studying. All young persons at this age are experiencing rapid growth in the physical, emotional, and academic areas coupled with the heightened peer pressures of the period. This combination leads to a zenith of pressure for all students that is even more severe for the LD youngsters. There is increased tension, frustration, and self-doubt as these students seek to deal with the special academic problems produced by the combination of learning disabilities and the usual adolescent concerns (Kutsick 1982).

The implication, then, is that LD adolescents need to be taught to use study skills as a means of coping with the demands placed upon them. The solution, however, does not seem to be that simple. In order to use such study skills, the learner must be able to control his or her metacognitive actions. Metacognition, according to Flavell (1976), refers to one's knowledge concerning one's own cognitive processes and products. These actions include the ability to predict, check, monitor, test, coordinate study attempts, and solve problems during the study process (Brown 1980). Deficiencies in these metacognitive skills can cause severe problems. Brown (1980) reports the following difficulties for all youngsters:

49

1. recognizing that problem difficulty has increased and that therefore there is a need for strategic intervention (Brown 1975);
2. using inferential reasoning to assess the probability that an assumption is true, given the information they already have (Brown 1978);
3. predicting the outcome of their attempts at strategy utilization both before and after the fact (Brown and Lawton 1977);
4. predicting the task difficulty in a variety of memory and problem-solving situations (Brown and Lawton 1977);
5. planning ahead in terms of strategic study-time apportionment (Brown and Compione 1977; Brown and Smiley 1978); and
6. monitoring the success of attempts to learn so that termination of such activities can be made when they are successful (and no longer necessary) or unsuccessful, so that new activities can be tried (Brown and Barclay 1976; Brown, Campione, and Barclay 1978).

In addition, Brown (1980) concludes that "in general, children fail to consider their behavior against sensible criteria, they follow instructions blindly, and they are deficient in self-questioning skills that would enable them to determine these inadequacies." All of these characteristics are more acute in LD students.

When these skills do emerge, they seem to come at later stages of development, sometimes not even by college age. Wong (1982) and Torgesen (1977) have researched the development of metacognitive skills with LD youngsters and have concluded that they indeed lack the ability to use self-checking skills and develop efficient study strategies, often giving up before exhausting all the possibilities that a task presents. The simple solution to successful study then becomes much more complex. The LD youngsters must be made aware of their present study habits, and they must know the options available to them to better these habits. Just as important, their teachers must be convinced of the facts that these skills are late in emerging even in normal youngsters, the skills must be taught, and some techniques have more use with some students and in some disciplines than others.

Help in these areas may be provided in a number of ways. The LD teacher may help the students in resource classes by aiding them in assessing their current study habits and strengthening their weak skills. This help may be done in the youngsters' content books to be most beneficial. The resource teacher may also work with content area teachers who have LD students in their classes to increase their awareness and get their cooperation in teaching study skills while determining the underlying demands of the assignments that they make. Both the resource teacher and content area teacher may work with parents to develop strategies that will help their children and reinforce what is being taught at school.

Helping learners evaluate the present status of their study skills requires little time and effort. There are several inventories available, but the Study Habits Checklist in Tables 6.1 and 6.2 by Kollaritsch (1981) exemplifies their content and can be used with LD students with minor modifications, particularly on items involving quotas such as #1, 3, and 8.

Table 6.1
Study Habits Checklist

R — Rarely
S — Sometimes   Name _____
G — Generally   Section _____
A — Always

Use the following checklist to see if you are regularly applying these techniques:

R S G A 1. Do you *read* and *learn* at the rate of at least 12–15 pp. per hour for history-type material?

R S G A 2. Do you read and study each day's assignments according to the *method by which you will be tested* — in fine detail or in generalities, or both?

R S G A 3. Can you regularly *concentrate* on your most difficult subject at peak efficiency for two hours without having to take a break?

R S G A 4. Do you regularly *ask* your professors for *help* or explanations when needed?

R S G A 5. Do you study for your difficult classes by reviewing first to yourself and then going over the material *out loud* with a student who is doing well in your class — approximately once a week?

R S G A 6. Do you occasionally compare your *lecture notes* with those of a good student from your class, to make sure you are not omitting important information and to see what they have recorded as main ideas, etc.?

R S G A 7. Do you *keep up* with *assignments* by studying every course at least a little every day?

R S G A 8. Do you *study* about *4 hours* (sometimes more) each day?

R S G A 9. Do you follow an efficient *schedule* that permits adequate time for study, recreation, and rest?

R S G A 10. Do you *work* as many *practice problems* as you have the time to do for all quantitative courses, such as math, physics, chemistry, and accounting?

R S G A 11. Do you make every effort to continue to develop your general English vocabulary, as well as to learn technical words from your areas of study?

R S G A 12. Do you *participate* in *class discussion*?

R S G A 13. Do you *visualize* what you are reading as you read — to improve comprehension and to ensure that you are concentrating?

R S G A 14. Do you analyze your *returned tests* to discover which part of a course you are losing the most points on — the lecture, text, outside reading, lab, etc.?

Table 6.1 (*cont.*)

R	S	G	A	15. Do you *correct* your mistakes?
R	S	G	A	16. Before exams do you review and attempt to *predict* test *questions according to the method by which you will be tested*?
R	S	G	A	17. Do you vary the rate at which you read and the reading method you use according to the difficulty and the purpose of the material?
R	S	G	A	18. Do you make an effort to become interested in and to study thoroughly, *all* your courses — not just those in your chosen field of study?
R	S	G	A	19. Do you study *primarily* with the goal of attaining knowledge, rather than for the grade?
R	S	G	A	20. Do you express yourself efficiently in *writing*?
R	S	G	A	21. Do you have *efficient review methods* and *test-taking techniques* for major examinations?
R	S	G	A	22. Do you have a satisfactory study *environment*?
R	S	G	A	23. Do you make an effort to *apply* the *knowledge* you gain, rather than merely memorizing facts?
R	S	G	A	24. Do you *complete assignments on time*?
R	S	G	A	25. Do you feel that your overall *grades are* or have been a fairly *accurate reflection* of your ability?
R	S	G	A	26. Are you able to *put aside personal problems* when you are trying to study?

Table from Kollaritsch (1981).

Another factor involved in this evaluation phase should be teacher evaluation. Not all LD adolescents will be helped by working on study skills. Deshler, Lowery, and Alley (1979) have concluded that the group who can be served include 89 percent of the youngsters with mild to moderate handicaps who possess the following characteristics:

1. reading level of at least third grade
2. facility with symbolic language
3. normal intelligence

Teachers must also be fully aware of the tasks involved in studying. As Towle's (1982) task analysis indicates (Table 6.3), the demands are numerous and complex. Youngsters have to be able to apply a wide variety of skills in order to study effectively.

Once LD adolescents and their teachers are aware of what skills the student has mastered to use in studying and what the tasks demand, there are a large number of study techniques available. Several are summarized in Table 6.4.

Table 6.2
Scoring Sheet For
Study Habits Checklist*

A = 3, G = 2, S = 1, R = 0

Total Possible Points: 78

Name _____

Section _____

Ranges						
Lowest	Below Average	Low Ave.	Mid Ave.	Hi Ave.	Above Average	Highest
0–8	9–24	25–36		37–52	53–68	69–78

0-8   = No doubt you won't pass!

9-24 = You probably won't pass!

25-36 = You are still in the danger zone!

37-52 = Substantial improvement can still be made!

53-68 = Good, but you can still improve in specific areas!

69-78 = Excellent! No improvement needed.

To Analyze Your Study Habits Test:

In the margins beside each item put a plus (+) if you have marked "A" or "G." Put a minus (−) if you have marked "S" or "R." Then count your minuses for each category listed below and give yourself a "satisfactory" or "unsatisfactory" for each category.

Number of Minuses

Category	A category should be marked unsatisfactory if you mark more than the following:
1. Reading Items — Nos. 1, 2, 3, 11, 13, 17	2
2. Study Habits — Nos. 4, 6, 7, 8, 10, 14, 15, 22, 24	4
3. Study Attitudes — Nos. 18, 19, 25, 26	1
4. General Study & Writing Skills — Nos. 5, 9, 12, 16, 20, 21, 23	3

*This test can be used as both a pre- and post-test.

Table from Kollaritsch (1981).

The commonalities of all these techniques are obvious — self-motivation through questioning, reading, reacting, reviewing — even though the particular sequence, emphasis, and format varies. While there are limited research data to prove the worth of these strategies and others (Anderson 1980), there are numerous success stories from teachers and parents. Part of this problem may be the difficulty in measuring something as internal and personal as studying, rather than the limited value of specific study

Table 6.3
Study Skills Analysis

Underlining	Take Notes from Print	Outlining from Print	Take Notes from Auditory
Can identify main concept	Can read material	Can read material	Knows vocabulary used in presentation
Can identify key terms	Uses readings & guide words	Can differentiate main points from supportive details	Can write/spell
Can identify supportive details	Uses summaries for main points	Uses section headings or questions from text to guide	Can paraphrase auditory input
Can use signal words to identify main points	Paraphrases text	Uses simple numeration system	Listens for specific information
	Uses signal words to identify key points	Identifies main points for outline	Recognizes organizational words
	Uses organizational format	Identifies subtopics for main points	Arranges information in sequences-time position
	Develops study questions to focus notes	Can outline single paragraphs	Uses nonverbal cues— pauses, gestures to identify information
	Takes notes from group of paragraphs	Can outline series of paragraphs	Writes key words
	Identifies main topics in notes to organize material		Writes in phrases
	Identifies subtopics in notes to organize facts		Reworks organization of notes
	Reworks notes		

techniques. The systematic use of good questions can be supported by research (Anderson 1980) and may be the key to success within each of these techniques, particularly if the key questions are directly related to explicit study criteria.

Availability, however, is not the major concern, since the appropriate techniques must be taught as a part of regular instruction, rather than remaining the "invisible . . . curriculum" (Towle 1982). The choice of techniques may vary from one subject to another, especially if the criteria for succeeding on assignments and tests are different. The absolute minimum requirements remain the same, in all cases, and may be summarized as follows: (1) LD youngsters *must* be taught a technique that is commensurate with their abilities. Instruction and task analysis, therefore, are always needed. (2) The same technique may not always work for every class, so each teacher or the resource teacher is responsible for teaching at least one method that will work in a particular class. (3) The youngsters must be

Table 6.4
Study Techniques

Technique	Steps	Author(s)	General
SQ3R	Survey, Question, Read, Recite, Review	Robinson	General, especially social studies and science (see Roe, Stoodt, and Burns 1983)
OK5R	Before: Overview; During: Key Ideas, Read, Record; After: Recite, Review, Correct	Pauk	General
C&S	Purpose, Question, Read, Additional ideas, Vocabulary, Additional questions, Study	Clary and Sheppo	General, especially for LD
C2R	Concentrate, Read, Remember	Moore	General
PQRST	Preview, Question, Read, Summarize, Test	Spache	Science (see Burmeister 1978)
REAP	Read, Encode, Annotate, Ponder	Eanet and Manzo	General (emphasis on writing)
PANORAMA	Purpose, Adapting rate to material, Need to pose questions, Overview, Read & Relate, Annotate, Memorize, Assess	Edwards	General
EVOKER	Explore, Vocabulary, Oral reading, Key ideas, Evaluate	Pauk	Literature (prose, poetry, drama)
SQRQCQ	Survey, Question, Read, Question, Compute, Question	Fay	Math

taught to monitor their own learning and realize when it is breaking down, in order to eventually become independent learners.

These facts mean that whatever technique is taught must be broken down into small structured steps that students fully understand and, after practice, can monitor for themselves. Bransford, Stein, and Vye (1982) have reported that less successful readers have superficial knowledge of assigned topics, their level of mastery of the subject, their readiness for tests, their need for rereading and further study through questioning, and their alternatives for retaining more information and understanding. All of these characteristics, obviously, relate to self-monitoring — the reader's knowing when there is a breakdown in learning. LD students, especially, must have a concrete way of learning to monitor themselves.

The easiest, simplest method of implementing the three absolute strategies mentioned above may be the use of two checklists, one for the teacher and one for the student. Using them forces the teacher to analyse the task and at least review a study strategy and also requires the student to analyse her/his performance of the task.

The checklist in Table 6.5 incorporates the major points that the teacher of LD adolescents needs to consider. Using it for major units of study should reduce much of the frustration of students and teachers. The checklist can be done mentally or in writing, although it would probably be best to write the information during initial trials.

LD students, too, should be taught to monitor their reading and study habits. While this practice will take extensive training, it is one of the few ways that these adolescents can achieve the independence that they must have for success. Use of the checklist on Table 6.6 for students, first in writing and later through silent review, can provide the structure needed for remembering the important and necessary points of study and successful reading.

A careful effort by teachers and students to use study techniques and habits such as these can help learning disabled adolescents overcome many of the characteristics that impede their ability to succeed in studying and learning independently. These procedures will help resolve some of the pressures of adolescence, as well as the academic problems produced by the learning disabilities. There is no one factor that will solve all these problems. However, awareness on the part of the teacher and the student; instruction and specific, structured help from the teacher; and use of heightened self-monitoring on the student's part should minimize an area that is otherwise very frustrating and defeating.

Table 6.5

Teacher Checklist

Many items based on Towle (1982)

Have I completed the following?

1. A mental or written task analysis of this assignment.

2. Prepared to review and/or build background before assigning.

3. Prepared to introduce and/or review the following vocabulary.

4. Reminded my students to study this information by using the
   _____ study technique.

5. Reminded my students that they will need to process this information by (check one or combination)
   observing
   listening
   reading

6. Suggested that my students organize this material by (check one or combination)
   underlining
   listing
   note taking (suggested technique _____)
   outlining
   questioning
   summarizing

7. Informed class to study for tests by (check one or combination)
   questioning me (written? oral?)
   question each other (written? oral?)
   paraphrasing (written? oral?)
   summarizing (written? oral?)
   writing answers that will show me that they can
   compare/contrast (topics:_____)
   draw conclusions (topics: _____)
   explain (topics: _____)
   list (topics: _____)
   diagram (topics:_____)
   draw timelines (topics: _____)
   demonstrate procedures (topics: _____)

8. Suggested initial reading of this material at a rate (check one)
   slow
   moderate
   rapid

Table 6.6
Student Checklist for Monitoring Reading

Before Reading

---

1. Do I know what the assignment is?

2. Have I looked over the assignment?

3. Do I need to ask someone to give me more background before I read?

4. Do I need to ask about vocabulary? List with page numbers.

         Words   Page

    _____   _____

    _____   _____

    _____   _____

    _____   _____

5. Do I have some questions to answer as I read?

    _____

    _____

    _____

6. Have I chosen an appropriate rate? (Slow, moderate, fast?)

*7. How am I going to organize this material? Check one or more.
    ____ underline
    ____ list
    ____ take notes
    ____ outline
    ____ ask myself questions
    ____ ask the teacher questions
    ____ retell aloud in my own words
    ____ write in my own words
    ____ write a practice exam question
    (check type)
    ____ compare/contrast
    ____ draw conclusions
    ____ explain
    ____ list
    ____ draw a diagram and explain
    ____ explain procedures

During Reading

---

1. Am I answering my questions?

2. Am I understanding what I read?

†3. When I don't understand, I will (choose one or more)
    ____ reread
    ____ jump ahead
    ____ use an outside reference (glossary, dictionary, map, etc.)
    ____ ask someone else
    ____ write down the questions to ask the teacher

Table 6.6 (*cont.*)

After Reading	
1. Have I answered my questions? List any I need to ask about.	Page

2. Have I organized the material in some way?

3. Am I ready to use this information by (check one)
   ___ reading the next assignment
   ___ solving problems
   ___ doing laboratory assignments
   ___ taking a test
   ___ writing a paper

*Items based on Towle (1982)
†Items based on Anderson (1980)

REFERENCES

Anderson, Thomas H. "Study Strategies and Adjunct Aids." In R. J. Spiro, B. Bruce, and W. F. Brewer, eds., *Theoretical Issues in Reading Comprehension*. Hillsdale, N.J.: Lawrence Erlbaum Associates, 1980.

Bransford, John D., Barry S. Stein, and Nancy J. Vye. "Helping Students Learn from Written Texts." In Martin H. Singer, ed., *Competent Reader, Disabled Reader: Research and Application*. Hillsdale, N.J.: Lawrence Erlbaum Associates, 1982.

Brown, Ann L. "Metacognitive Development and Reading." In R. J. Spiro, B. Bruce, and W. F. Brewer, eds., *Theoretical Issues in Reading Comprehension*. Hillsdale, N.J.: Lawrence Erlbaum Associates, 1980.

Burmeister, Lou E. *Reading Strategies for Middle and Secondary School Teachers*, 2nd ed. Reading, Mass.: Addison-Wesley, 1978.

Clary, L. M., and K. G. Sheppo. "New Research and Ideas for Learning Disabilities Teachers." In William M. Cruickshank and Eli Tash, eds., *Academics and Beyond, Vol. 4, The Best of ACLD*. Syracuse: Syracuse University Press, 1983.

Deshler, D. D., N. Lowery, and G. R. Alley. "Programming Alternatives for Learning Disabled Adolescents: A Nationwide Survey." *Academic Therapy,* 14 (1979): 389–397.

Eanet, Marilyn G., and Anthony V. Manzo. "REAP—A Strategy for Improving Writing/Study Skills." *Journal of Reading,* 29 (1976): 647–652.

Edwards, Peter. "Panorama: A Study Technique." *Journal of Reading,* 16 (1973): 132–135.

Fay, Leo. "Reading Study Skills: Math and Science." In J. A. Figurel, ed., *Reading and Inquiry.* Newark, Del.: International Reading Association, 1965.

Flavell, J. H. "Metacognitive Aspects of Problem Solving." In L. B. Resnick, ed., *The Nature of Intelligence.* Hillsdale, N.J.: Lawrence Erlbaum Associates, 1976.

Kollaritsch, Jane. *Reading and Study Organization Methods for Higher Learning,* rev. ed. Columbus, Ohio: Komo Associates, 1981.

Kronick, Doreen. "The Learning Disabled Adult. " *Learning Times* 16, no. 4 (1982): 1, 3, 6.

Kutsick, Koressa. "Remedial Strategies for Learning Disabled Adolescents." *Academic Therapy* 17 (1982): 329–335.

Moore, Mary A. C2R: "Concentrate, Read, Remember." *Journal of Reading* 24 (1981): 337–339.

Pauk, Walter. *How to Study in College,* 2nd. ed. Boston: Houghton Mifflin, 1974.

———. "On Scholarship: Advice to High School Students." *The Reading Teacher* 17 (1963): 73–78.

Robinson, F. P. *Effective Study,* rev. ed. New York: Harper and Row, 1961.

Roe, Betty D., Barbara Stoodt, and Paul Burns. *Secondary School Reading Instruction: The Content Areas,* 2nd ed. Boston: Houghton Mifflin, 1983.

Torgesen, Joseph K. "Memorization Processes in Reading-disabled Children." *Journal of Educational Psychology* 69 (1977): 571–578.

Towle, Maxine. "Learning How to be a Student When You Have a Learning Disability." *Journal of Learning Disabilities* 15 (1982): 90–93.

Wong, Bernice. "Strategic Behaviors in Selecting Retrieval Cues in Gifted, Normal Achieving and Learning Disabled Children." *Journal of Learning Disabilities* 15 (1982): 33–37.

7

Beyond Academics
Programming for
Young Learning Disabled Adults

William C. Adamson, Dorothy F. Ohrenstein, Samuel Fiederer

THIS IS A PRESENTATION of a one year follow-up of a multi-dimensional program for young adult males (19 to 35 years of age) developed by Group Growth Services, Inc. The services are built around group processes for young male adults and their parents, liaison with vocational training centers, small group tutoring, and life survival and independent living skills.

More specifically, the program is designed to meet the needs of an LD population with problems in low self-esteem, poor socialization skills, prolonged dependency on parents, delay in development of vocational skills, and academic "softness" or regression in reading and mathematics which limit level of entry into the occupational market.

Currently, there is no one program in the Delaware Valley which has been designed to meet *all* these needs of this young adult population.

In a very real way, Group Growth Services has been a pioneering agency blazing a new trail for the young people it is serving; men and women who were the first generation identified as LD children to reach young adulthood.

Dr. Sheldon Rappaport, and a farsighted board of directors, organized the Pathway School for children with learning problems in the Delaware Valley in 1961. Group Growth Services has picked up two graduates of that school who are now in their mid-twenties.

Since the advent of the Education for All Handicapped Children Act (1977) and the enactment of Public Law 94-142, hundreds of thousands of school age children are being identified as LD children and being included in prescriptive education through the secondary school level.

Few community services are being developed to meet the needs of this enormous population as it moves into young adulthood. We feel that Group Growth Services represents a viable model to meet this unprecedented challenge.

MULTIDIMENSIONAL PROGRAM

During the past two years our Group Growth Services, Inc. has been providing services to eight young LD adult males and their families. We have referred to these services as a multidimensional program, including the following eight dimensions:

Dimension 1. Group psychotherapy

Monthly group psychotherapy experience for the young adults. Role playing and psychodrama techniques to enhance personal and social development. Group discussion sessions last about two hours and discussions are initiated by young adults and by group leaders.

Dimension 2. Concurrent group sessions for parents

Monthly group sessions for parents. Group cohesion and group support allows full range of emotional expression for parents.

The use of a monthly newsletter or bulletin highlights some of the plans and profiles for each family throughout succeeding months.

Dimension 3. Group socialization and recreational experiences

Monthly meetings focused on socialization and recreation including bowling, informal parties, attendance at football games, visiting programs in which parents may be actively involved in their life work, and family recreation days at the local park or at the summer home of one of the parents. These family recreational experiences are designed approximately four times a year.

Dimension 4. Individual psychotherapy

The use of individual psychotherapy once every four to six weeks to allow project director to talk on a very personal and intimate basis with each one of the young adults. Discussion focuses on their feelings about the total group process and about aspects of their family and family living. Also, they are able to work on looking at their own self-awareness and awareness of others and their relationship between themselves and others.

Dimension 5. Individual parent or couple counseling

All parents are seen individually or together approximately every four weeks. In addition, the social worker carries a strong tie and liaison to each family and is very available by telephone.

Discussions are focused on the personal and intimate details of the young adult's relationship with parents and with family, with specific focus on those issues relating to fostering independence.

Dimension 6. Active liaison with community vocational services

A very close tie and liaison has been established with all of the agencies serving our clients. We have visited the programs and have regular telephone contacts when indicated. The purpose is to ensure a consistent and integrated approach to the clients.

Dimension 7. Active tutoring, technical training and formal classroom learning

All adults in the project have been evaluated in terms of math skills, reading levels, and spelling skills. All are involved, as indicated, in group tutoring once a week.

Dimension 8. Cooperative apartment living and life survival skills training

The ultimate goal is to help each of the young adults to be able to move into living apart from his/her own family. A great deal of the group work is focused on developing the skills necessary for survival apart from the family.

MULTIDISCIPLINE PROFESSIONAL STAFF

This program has been developed and facilitated by a multidisciplinary staff consisting of a psychiatrist, social worker, educational psychologist, special educational teacher, physical educational teacher, and a language development specialist.

The psychiatrist has provided leadership for Dimensions 1 and 4, namely Group and Individual Psychotherapy. In *the monthly group ses-*

sions each individual is encouraged to bring his past and current social experiences into the group. The ongoing group support, the identification and transference processes with co-leaders of the group, and the success of working through old problems in new ways, raises the self-esteem of the members of the group. Old narcissistic wounds, often associated with years of failure and with specific learning disabilities, are partially healed, and new ventures and new risks are undertaken in social and vocational areas with greater self-confidence.

Content for these group sessions has included discussions on Money Management, Budgeting, Developing Life Survival/Independent Living Skills, and Why and How of Dating, and Growing into Manhood.

In the Individual Psychotherapy the Board Certified psychiatrist talks with each young adult on a personal and intimate basis every four or six weeks. Each young man is encouraged to discuss his feelings about the group, to talk about aspects of his family and family living, as well as the new relationships with men and women coming into his life. An attempt is made to help the young man understand the nature of the processes which go on between himself and others, and to learn from past experiences new ways of coping with these experiences as part of his new life. A major emphasis is put on looking at the total family dynamics and the kinds of things which the young adult sets in motion in the family, as well as the motives for setting up such a reaction and interaction.

The social worker has special skills directed toward Dimensions 2, 5, and 6. Briefly, the social worker does four things. She participates with the psychiatrist in the diagnosis and evaluation of family functioning in the initial evaluation, to determine whether the young man will fit into the group, and whether the family will fit into the parent group.

Secondly, she facilitates the group meetings with parents once a month. Thirdly, she provides liaison with the vocational settings, and fourthly, she works with individual parents.

In the area of services to parents, the underlying philosophy is one of understanding parents in the context of the emotional impact of having a child with a handicap or disability. The dynamics are similar regardless of the disability. Parents experience a sense of loss of the fantasized normal child. Feelings of chronic sorrow are triggered at times when parents become aware again of the contrast between what is and what might have been.

In the *diagnostic process* it is essential to learn about the parents' experiences and feelings related to diagnosis and finding institutions and professional people to help them and their child. The past lives in the present and it colors their view of the present. It is necessary for our understanding of parents and for our appreciation of their experience to learn about their journey. The diagnostic process for us becomes one of mutual choice. We choose them for our groups and they choose us as partners in behalf of their sons' growth.

Group sessions for parents are held monthly. They are unstructured and last for one hour and forty-five minutes. The major benefits have been to provide an environment where parents of similar experiences and concerns can share their concerns, gain support, feel less isolated and learn from each other. There have been three major themes in the sessions.

1. Past experiences related to the struggles in searching for a diagnosis and in finding appropriate educational programs and helpful professionals.
2. The day by day incidents, frustrations, joys, struggles, conflicts with the accompanying feelings of sorrow, helplessness, hope for change and the fear of hoping, and particularly the pain of the child's failures or possible failures.
3. Concerns for the future.

In *individual parent or couple counseling* parents are seen together or individually once a month. Some parents are seen in individual therapy or couples therapy as well. The degree of involvement is determined by need and contracted for.

The focus for professional intervention with parents is as follows:

1. Offsetting parental feelings of helplessness.
2. Helping parents set realistic expectations and goals for their sons, looking at chronological age, mental age, social age and emotional age in a prospective of normal development.
3. Helping parents understand that their sons' delays in academic, social and emotional development means that they will need a longer time to master the tasks of adolescence and to achieve independence and maturity. They are on a different time schedule.
4. Helping parents with their conflicts over the wish to foster independence and the need to protect their vulnerable child.

The last issue has been the most central focus for intervention. Ways must be found, with gentleness and consistency, and with respect for the parents' feelings to support them in beginning to let go of their natural and powerful need to be protective of their vulnerable young adult-child in order to allow growth toward independence to take place. At the same time they need to be supported in being able to tolerate the fears they have of the child's possible failure, the possibility he may be hurt emotionally, and to bear the child's pain and their own pain in the face of failure. The goal must be separation from family and independence.

The fundamental aspect of *group socialization experiences* is to make the presentation as practical and viable as possible. Group social situations are geared toward participation. To prolong the "spectator" stage of these young men could mean continuing a catastrophe. The "program" is movement and verbalization.

If "push" is needed, we push—cautiously!

Spirit has to be developed and, at times, almost picked up, in a figurative sense, from the floor. You cannot sermonize. They are prone, then, to see you within the framework of a parental figure against whom there is frequently much antagonism. At the same time, certain limits must be set up to contain impulsive tendencies, much as you might expect with much younger persons. The emotions, the feelings, the conflicts, are often early teenage.

The emphasis within the group socialization experience is not to overpower any of the individuals in the group, or the group as a whole. Therefore, it is important not to enhance negative roles already felt in relationship to earlier failures. Positive leadership support and group support and cohesion become the forces which shape the age-appropriate behaviors and the socially acceptable roles.

"The Party" is one of our major strategies and we have such a party at least once within every two month period. For these parties, we have carefully selected several attractive young women counselors who can talk to, dance with, and generally relate to the young men heretofore "scared to death" of girls. While these young counselors have been chosen, in part, for their attractiveness and intelligence, within the framework of a group, their role is never to be girlfriend. Certainly, this creates a somewhat unrealistic aspect since some of the young men become attracted to them.

All of our current counselors are young ladies who now function as part of the group. They are professional teachers who can go through all the roles of leader, never mother, as well as friend. They are aware from their teaching experience of a need for a "necessary separation" that will not create psychological turmoil or guilt in themselves or the young men.

The important happening is that these formally "unsocialized" males can now talk in a frank manner to a "girl", other than their mother or sister, about all kinds of subjects. These are real girls in every sense of the word, untouchable, but reachable. There is a host of openly verbalized feelings brought out in the parties through dancing, singing, story telling and the recounting of successes and failures. At the same time highly individualized problems that do not relate to the group are carefully avoided and held over for the individual counseling sessions.

The food served at the parties has become a fascinating gauge for evaluation of the success of the group's interaction. What used to be a stimulus for concentrated stares and impulsive lunges is more or less taken for granted. It can now be casually introduced, displayed for a time, or held back without creating problems. Nevertheless, the nurturing impact of the food is not to be overlooked. Food is a stimulant, and a device in the re-direction of topics, mood, or unique situations. The program goes on while the food is served and consumed. It never really stops. Acceleration of interaction, social awareness, and group cohesion, are hoped for achievements of the parties, plus the need for the group to keep moving, and to occasionally "switch gears" while continuing that movement.

The introduction of the parents to some of the parties, family picnics, ball games, and other events is now becoming a further involvement and significant development. The young men who, in many cases, saw what they believed to be rejection by their parents compounding their own feelings of self-rejection, are now reaching out and re-establishing a closeness that is warm and rewarding. What is doubly rewarding is to see how sensitively the parents are responding.

8

Learning Disabilities
and Social Skill Development
Research-Based Implications
for the Developmental Life Span

Paul J. Gerber and Rhonda H. Kelley

SINCE THE FIELD of learning disabilities has begun to grapple with the concept of life-long learning and life adjustment (Wiederholt 1981), the area of social skills development becomes increasingly more important. Kronick (1978) has pointed out that problems in social skills are probably more disabling in total life functioning than academic problems. Similarly, Johnson and Myklebust (1976) have observed that select social problems in learning disabled (LD) individuals can be the most debilitating of the learning disorders because they impede acquisition of basic adaptive patterns of behavior.

As the social problems of learning disabled individuals become a priority issue in the field, it is obvious that professionals and parents must begin to adopt new methodologies and approaches to facilitate research and then employ appropriate diagnostic and prescriptive strategies. For this reason the concept of developmental life span psychology (Schell and Hall 1983) becomes an attractive and practical framework in which to study social skill development through the stages of the human life cycle. Those in the field of learning disabilities are intimately aware of the dearth of research in social skills during the years of LD expansion. Now, there is a body of research literature from which we can gain much insight. However, only when the research is placed on a developmental continuum are we able to view emerging patterns that may significantly impact programming and delivery of services. By looking at the literature of social skills development of learning disabled individuals in childhood, adolescence, and adulthood, one is able to gain a unique perspective—one which emphasizes the dynamic elements of social skills as one stage of growth leads to another.

SOCIAL SKILL DEVELOPMENT IN LEARNING DISABLED CHILDREN

Prior to formal efforts in the research of this area within learning disabilities, numerous clinical observations were made about the social abilities and disabilities of learning disabled children. Kahn (1969) observed that the perceptual inadequacies of LD children when applied to interpersonal relationships involve inaccurate perception and conceptualization of social-personal matters. Kronick (1969) believed that LD children had distortion of perceptual information which caused impaired feedback and which in turn caused disorganization of life space. Further, Lewis, Strauss, and Lehtinen (1960) stated that the mechanism that organizes behavior and helps the child perceive social situations and develop awareness fails to operate properly. Summing up, Wender (1971) keenly observed that the LD child is an unsuccessful extrovert.

PEER STATUS

One familiar body of research literature relative to the social skills of LD children involves peer status. As early as 1950, Johnson investigated the social position of a population of fourth and fifth grade children similar to LD and found them to be rejected more and accepted less than their nonhandicapped peers. Whereas he expected the cause to be low academic ability, he surprisingly found that social and interpersonal skills were the problems. He hypothesized that these inappropriate behaviors were compensatory behaviors stemming from self-conceptual problems.

More recently, there have been other investigations into peer status. Bryan (1974) found that LD boys were twice as likely to be ignored by their peers and teachers than their nondisabled classmates. This study was replicated in 1976 by Bryan and similar results were found. Siperstein, Bopp, and Bak (1978) investigated the social positions of fifth and sixth grade LD children and found that they were less popular than nondisabled children. Bruininks (1978) found similar results when studying LD children in mainstream programs. Moreover, she found that LD students were less accurate in assessing his own personal status in the group.

PROBLEMS IN NONVERBAL BEHAVIORAL CUE INTERPRETATION

Problems in perceiving and comprehending nonverbal cues of behavior have been written about by various clinicians. Kronick (1972) reported a cluster of problems stemming from difficulty in nonverbal cues in space and perceiving social situations as a *gestalt*. Moreover, she cited misuse of body expression, difficulty in interpreting people's nonverbal messages, inability to understand the full impact of messages on others, and inability to monitor one's impact on others in conversation or social interaction as some of the major problems (p. 69).

Through studies in this area, one is able to fully appreciate this problem as it relates to LD children. Emery (1975) found that LD children ages 7 to 12 were less accurate than controls in understanding facial expressions. Serafica (1979) saw a significant difference in LD children when they were asked to identify and comprehend visual social cues like facial expressions and body postures as well as auditory social cues like tone of voice. Bryan (1979) found similar problems in interpreting nonverbal cues but stressed that more subtle cues (as opposed to gross movements) posed the greatest problems for correct interpretation. Overall, LD children were less accurate than their peers in comprehension of nonverbal communication.

Two other studies of different dimensions are relevant within this section. Gerber and Zinkgraf (1982) found in a comparative study that 6 and 7 year old and 10 and 11 year old learning disabled children are two to three years behind their nondisabled peers in social perceptual ability. Simply put, they were unable to integrate a complex of visual cues and interpret attitude relationships, roles, and the subsequent probabilities of action. The investigators also related that the data showed an increase in social perceptual ability with age. This led to the hypothesis that LD children may be experiencing a lag not a deficit in this developmental area.

In another study, Bryan (1978) showed videotapes of LD and control children to strangers. After viewing the videotaped behavioral vignettes, raters were able to discriminate the LD subjects from the control subjects. The kinesics and proxemics of the LD children were easily discernible.

SOCIAL SKILLS OF LEARNING DISABLED ADOLESCENTS

An examination of the social skills literature of the LD adolescent reveals that there is a variation on a theme related at the outset of this paper. Writing on the ultimate implications of this problem, Alley and Deshler (1978) have pointed out that problems in social adjustment and social perception of the LD adolescent could potentially be more of a hindrance to success in life adjustment than academic problems. Kronick (1972) and Siegel (1972), writing about the clinical aspects of LD adolescence, have cited misuse in body expression, trouble interpreting nonverbal messages, and improper monitoring of self-behavior as major problems. Kronick has written: "It is almost as if the learning disabled adolescent were deaf and blind for several years, and were then suddenly thrust into a culture wherein he is expected to have mastered incredibly complex communication patterns, most of which have been internalized by others and are practiced unconsciously" (p. 69). Similar to the literature on the LD child, the majority of the studies do fall into the general categories of peer status and problems in nonverbal behavioral cue interpretation.

PEER STATUS AND SELF-CONCEPT

In order to add more specificity to the peer status dynamics of LD adolescents (especially at a time in which peer status is particularly important), an important study has been reported. Schumaker, Sheldon-Wilgren, and Sherman (1980) studied LD adolescents attending regular classes. Generally, they have found that LD junior high students are not isolates in the regular classroom. They were found to engage in conversation with as many different peers as their nondisabled peers and actually spend more time in discussion than their nondisabled peers. Moreover, the researchers reported that "peers were not found to ignore their initiations much more often than they ignore the non-LD students' initiations" (p. 60). Rosenberg and Gaier (1977) linked low peer acceptance and self-concept. They found that comparative scores on ratings of self were lower for the LD adolescent. From this they concluded that LD youngsters are stigmatized and perceived to be less desirable because of these deficits.

PROBLEMS IN NONVERBAL BEHAVIORAL CUE INTERPRETATION

There are a number of studies in this area of investigation which generally supports the notion that problems in LD childhood are carried over to LD adolescence. Wiig and Harris (1974) showed videotapes to adolescent females matched on IQ, race, sex, and socioeconomic status. Examples of the nonverbal expressions in the videotapes were anger, fear, joy, love, and embarrassment. Results showed that the LD adolescents were less accurate than controls quantitatively and qualitatively in labeling emotions. Furthermore, they often took relatively positive emotions and misperceived them as negative emotions.

Pearl and Cosden (1982) studied 88 children in junior high school to assess their social perceptual ability. Learning disabled and nondisabled adolescents were shown soap opera sequences and then were tested on their comprehension of character interactions. Findings suggested that the LD group made more comprehension errors. Perhaps of greater significance was the commentary made from clinical observations. The authors believed that their findings support the hypothesis "that the LD individual's social problems may be due in part to their difficulty in understanding important information that is subtly or implicitly conveyed in social interactions" (p. 372).

In another study, Bachara (1976) investigated empathic ability in LD adolescents. After listening to a story, subjects were asked to choose the salient emotion of the main character. Deficiencies were noted in ability to empathize with others and in perceiving social situations correctly.

SOCIAL SKILLS OF LEARNING DISABLED ADULTS

While there is currently a dearth of information on the LD adult, there is a small collection of studies that allow insight into social skill problems as they are experienced in life adjustment settings rather than educational settings. Perhaps the research that has the greatest potential effect are the follow-up studies done on one-time school diagnosed LD problems. Without a doubt, they give firm warning and indication of the social skills problems that persist throughout development.

Several studies done in the 1960s gave a mixed review of social functioning of subjects who once had problems now equated with learning disabilities. Balow and Blomquist (1965) followed up a small sample of 32 former reading clinic clients and their psychological profiles revealed social and emotional difficulties. Rawson (1968) performed a follow-up study of 56 males of which 36 were diagnosed dyslexic. All subjects were from high socioeconomic brackets and the average IQ was 131. Results showed that most of the young adults in this study had made successful social adjustments.

In another study, Hardy (1968) studied the social and vocational adjustment of 40 formally dyslexic students. Satisfactory vocational adjustment (in semi-skilled and unskilled jobs) was noted in the formally dyslexic group, but unsatisfactory social adjustment was noted as compared to the control group. Hardy concluded that reading problems did not seem to influence vocational and social adjustment.

Revealing insights of social skills problems were described in the Lehtinen-Rogan and Hartman (1976) classic follow-up study of a former

Cove School population. Interesting clinical information was revealed via the administration of the Minnesota Multiphasic Inventory (MMPI) to 70 percent of their follow-up population. They described a variety of problems in LD adults.

1. They feel responsible to form themselves into likable and successful people but find it hard to do so.
2. They find social relationships trying. They want and need people but lack the confidence that people can like or respect them.
3. There is a "substantial tendency" to move between despondency and euphoria in social relationships because there is an underlying level of depression which is lifted by social contact.
4. They are very sensitive and easily hurt while being tense and anxious from their condition. (pp. 85–86)

In the summary statement of their study, Lehtinen-Rogan and Hartman emphasized an inability of the LD adult to form close personal relationships, low self-esteem, poor coping with tension, and variability in mood.

Some of these characteristics and attributes were noted by Patton and Polloway (1981) in their investigation into the salient issues facing the LD adult. They uncovered problems and clustered them into the following:

1. *personal*—disorganization, sloppiness, carelessness, difficulty in following directions, poor decision-making skills, inadequate independent functioning skills
2. *emotional*—frustration, anxiety, fear, anger, sense of helplessness, guilt, poor self-concept, embarrassment, neurotic or borderline psychotic symptoms
3. *social*—social imperception, poor peer relationships, problems in reacting to people and situations appropriately, problems in adaptive functioning
4. *psychological*—impulsivity, restlessness, hyperactivity (p. 83)

Finally, Blalock (1980) wrote about clinical findings of her work with 38 clients ages 17 to 37 in her clinic at Northwestern University. She related that select individuals show a diversity of social problems. Her observations corroborated several of the studies described in the childhood and adolescence parts of this paper.

Blalock wrote that one of the biggest problems is social perception — ranging from mild to severe forms. Thus, her clients were described as having few friends, saying inappropriate comments, and inappropriately using personal space in social behavior. They also had trouble following rapidly shifting conversations, maintained poor eye contact, and did not respond to social cues. Overall, she admitted that those clients with problems in social perception simply did not realize that they turned people off. This was almost the exact observation of Siegel (1966) in writing about the LD adolescent.

DISCUSSION

An examination of the literature on social skills in LD individuals reveals that there are similar problems across developmental stages. Despite Alley and Deshler's (1979) warning that adolescents may not share the same attributes of younger LD children, it seems that in the case of social skills development that evidence leads to the opposite conclusion. Certainly, Blalock (1980) adds credence to this position when she speaks of the assorted "persisting problems" she sees in her LD adult clinic. Also, it becomes more apparent that there is a deficit in social skills development rather than a lag (Gerber and Zinkgraf 1981). Learning disabled individuals just do not seem to attain full mastery in social skills development.

The literature suggests that there are several problem areas that extend throughout the developmental continuum and evidence themselves as significant life adjustment problems. The most notable problems are generally clustered in the broad areas of social perceptual skills and peer relations. More specifically, it is obvious that there are dramatic problems integrating high-level verbal and nonverbal cues and responding appropriately to the ongoing signals of a social interaction. Without question, there are other problems yet uncovered and others that need greater specificity.

What becomes obvious from this review is that social skills development should be an important agenda item for the field of learning disabilities. Problems in social adjustment should not be viewed as a set of dynamics which are the secondary effects of academic failure. They, at best, should be approached with equal emphasis (Cronin and Gerber 1982) in childhood and share top priority in adolescence with vocational skill development.

Finally, with the realization that LD adults possess problems in social and emotional functioning, it is incumbent that systems be devised to address these life-long needs. The field must continue to break away from its traditional focus on education as the centerpiece of treatment, and human service delivery systems need to gear up for this "new type of client."

76   GERBER AND KELLEY

REFERENCES

Alley, G., and D. Deshler. *Teaching the Learning Disabled Adolescent: Strategies and Methods.* Denver: Love, 1979.

Bachara, G. H. "Empathy in Learning Disabled Children." *Perceptual and Motor Skills* 43 (1976): 541–542.

Balow, B., and M. Blomquist. "Young Adults Ten to Fifteen Years after Severe Reading Disability." *Journal of Special Education* 6, no. 4 (1972): 397–409.

Blalock, J. W. "Persistent Problems and Concerns of Young Adults with Learning Disabilities." In W. M. Cruickshank and A. Silver, eds., *Bridges to Tomorrow: Vol. 2, The Best of ACLD.* Syracuse: Syracuse University Press, 1981.

Bruininks, V. L. "Peer Status and Personality Characteristics of Learning Disabled and Nondisabled Students." *Journal of Learning Disabilities* (1978): 29–34.

Bryan T. "Learning Disabled Children's Comprehension of Nonverbal Communication." *Journal of Learning Disabilities* 10 (1977): 36–41.

———. "Peer Popularity of Learning Disabled Children." *Journal of Learning Disabilities* 7 (1974): 621–625.

———. "Peer Popularity of Learning Disabled Children." *Journal of Learning Disabilities* 9 (1976): 307–311.

Bryan, T., and J. Bryan. *Understanding Learning Disabilities,* 2nd ed. Sherman Oaks, Cal.: Alfred, 1978.

Cronin, M. E., and P. J. Gerber. "Preparing the Learning Disabled Adolescent for Adulthood." *Topics in Learning and Learning Disabilities* 2, no. 3 (1983): 55–68.

Emery, E. J. "Social Perception Processes in the Normal and Learning Disabled Children." Doctoral dissertation, Southern Illinois University, 1975.

Gerber, P. J. "A Study of Social Perceptual Ability in Learning Disabled and Nonhandicapped Children." Doctoral dissertation, University of Michigan, 1978.

Gerber, P. J., and S. Zinkgraf. "A Comparative Study of Social Perceptual Ability in Learning Disabled and Nonhandicapped Children." *Learning Disability Quarterly* 5, no. 4 (1982): 374–378.

Hardy, M. "Clinical Follow-up Study of Disabled Readers." Doctoral dissertation, University of Toronto, 1968.

Johnson, G. O. "A Study of the Social Position of Mentally Retarded Children in Regular Grades." *American Journal of Mental Deficiency* 55 (1950): 60–89.

Johnson, D., and H. Myklebust. *Learning Disabilities: Educational Principles and Practices.* New York: Grune and Stratton, 1967.

Kahn, J. P. "Emotional Concomitants of the Brain-damaged Child." *Journal of Learning Disabilities* 2 (1969): 644–651.

Kronick, D. *What about Us? The LD Adolescent.* San Rafael, Cal.: Academic Therapy, 1975.

Lehtinen-Rogan, L. L., and L. A. Hartman. *A Follow-up Study of Learning Disabled Children as Adults.* Final Report (Project No. 443CH60010, Grant No. OEG-0-74-7453). Washington, D.C.: Bureau of Education for the Handicapped, U.S. Department of Health, Education and Welfare, 1976.

Lewis, R. S., A. A. Strauss, and L. L. Lehtinen. *The Other Child.* New York: Grune and Stratton, 1960.

Patton, J. R., and E. A. Polloway. "The Learning Disabled: The Adult Years." *Topics in Learning and Learning Disabilities* 2, no. 3 (1983): 79–88.

Rawson, M. *Developmental Language Disability: Adult Accomplishments of Dyslexic Boys.* Baltimore: Johns Hopkins University Press, 1968.

Rosenberg, B. S., and E. L. Gaier. "The Self-Concept of the Adolescent with Learning Disabilities." *Adolescence* 12 (1977): 489–498.

Schell, R. E., and E. Hall. *Developmental Psychology Today,* 4th ed. New York: Random House, 1983.

Schumaker, J. B., J. Sheldon-Wildgen, and J. A. Sherman. *An Observational Study of the Academic and Social Behavior of Learning Disabled Adolescents in the Regular Classroom* (Research Report No. 22). Lawrence: University of Kansas Institute for Research in Learning Disabilities, 1980.

Serafica, R. C., and N. I. Harway. "Social Relations and Self-esteem of Children with Learning Disabilities." *Journal of Clinical Child Psychology* 8 (1979): 227–233.

Siegel, E. *The Exceptional Child Grows Up.* New York: E. P. Dutton, 1974.

Siperstein, G. N., J. J. Bopp, and J. J. Bak. *Social Status of Learning Disabled Children.* Cambridge, Mass.: Research Institute for Educational Problems, 1977.

Wender, H. *Minimal Brain Damage in Children.* New York: Wiley-Interscience, 1976.

Wiederholt, J. L., ed. "Life-span Instruction for the Learning Disabled." *Topics in Learning and Learning Disabilities* 2, no. 3 (1982): 1–88.

Wiig, E. H., and S. P. Harris. "Perception and Interpretation of Nonverbally Expressed Emotions by Adolescents with Learning Disabilities." *Perceptual and Motor Skills* 38 (1974): 239–245.

9

An Integrated System for Providing Content to Learning Disabled Adolescents Using an Audio-Taped Format

Jean B. Schumaker, Donald D. Deshler, Pegi H. Denton

THE PROBLEMS encountered by learning disabled students in secondary schools are often magnified by the complex set of curricular demands placed on students at that level. These demands are particularly taxing for the LD student who is placed in mainstreamed classes for the majority of the school day. Recent studies indicate that adolescents are mainstreamed for more than four periods a day (Brandis and Halliwell 1980; Deshler, Lowrey, and Alley 1979). The LD student's success in the secondary mainstreamed setting is largely a function of his or her ability to acquire and deal effectively with the content delivered in regular classes. Unlike the elementary setting where the instructional emphasis is on basic skill mastery, the emphasis in secondary schools shifts to content acquisition in different subject areas. Because of their poor skills in reading, writing, listening, and notetaking, LD students are particularly prone to fall behind their peers in a relatively short period of time, and this heightens the probability of behavior-related problems, such as acting out, absenteeism, or even dropping out of school.

Although much of the instruction delivered to LD students in resource room settings is designed to help them acquire skills beneficial to their success in the regular class, this instruction is often insufficient or inappropriately designed to allow students to effectively cope with the complex curriculum demands of the regular class (Wiederholt and McEntire 1980). The demands placed on adolescents in secondary schools are very diverse and, especially for the underachieving student, very stringent. In regular classes, LD students are expected to meet many of the same curriculum demands placed on all students. They must be able to learn, integrate, manipulate, and express large amounts of content information in spite of their handicapped condition. The following is a list of specific features that cause great difficulty for learning disabled populations. First, the majority of secondary-level classes place heavy emphasis on reading assignments as a means for students to acquire content information. Typically, teachers present major ideas and sample problems during class periods and assign students to read related and supportive material from textbooks. Frequently, homework assignments involve reading assignments. It is not uncommon for classes to cover as much as fifty textbook pages per week in a regular class. Second, most textbooks used in secondary classes are written at or above the designated grade level (Carlson 1979). Given that the average reading level of learning disabled adolescents in high school ranges from third to fifth grade (Alley and Deshler 1979; Warner, Schumaker, Alley, and Deshler 1980), few LD students can benefit from the information presented in their texts. Consequently, reading assignments often go unread, and attendant homework assignments based on the readings are not completed. Thus, the result is poor grades. Third, many regular-class teachers in secondary schools assume that all students have sufficient reading skills to allow them to master the content presented in the classroom textbooks. These teachers see their primary role as that of delivering academic content and not of teaching reading skills. Consequently, students rarely receive any skill instruction within the regular classroom after the elementary grades. This absence of basic skill instruction may be a contributing factor to the plateauing effect in reading achievement noted by Warner et al. (1980), who studied LD adolescents' academic skills. Fourth, in order to successfully complete the requirements for high school graduation within a four-year period, students must be enrolled in a minimum of four classes per semester. Typically, most of the classes make major reading demands on students. The failure and frustration that a learning disabled adolescent feels in attempting to deal with reading assignments beyond his or her skill level are compounded when assignments from several classes accumulate. Finally, information that is presented orally to students (either through lectures or taped materials) is often poorly organized and ineffectively presented (e.g., main points are not stressed, advance organizers are not used, repetitions are not made) (Moran 1980), thus increasing the difficulty experienced by the LD adolescent with listening skill deficits.

Several solutions have been offered to help meet the demands faced by LD students in mainstreamed secondary classes. The most commonly offered solution is to provide LD students with resource room assistance for the purpose of teaching them reading skills that will allow them to better deal with the reading demands in the regular classroom; however, at this time there is limited documentation as to the effectiveness of such remedial instruction in appreciably raising the reading levels of learning disabled students in secondary schools (Deshler et al. 1979). Thus, resource room instruction designed to increase the student's reading facility not only frequently falls short of that goal, but at the same time presents another problem by removing the student from one or more regular classes for the purpose of the resource room instruction. The LD student is expected to make up for the time away from the regular class by "reading" the textbook assignment. It is ironic that very little instructional time in resource settings is devoted to teaching LD students skills related to their deficits in listening comprehension, information organization and manipulation, etc., given the large demand for these skills in the regular classroom.

Another frequently proposed solution to help LD students meet the demands of the secondary setting is to have the learning disability teacher in the resource room tutor the LD student in the content delivered in the regular classroom. This solution is inappropriate for several reasons (Alley and Deshler 1979) but mostly because LD teachers are not certified to deliver regular classroom content. Furthermore, such an approach is at best a short-term solution for the student in that the student is not taught strategies for more independent learning.

A third solution is to teach LD students a strategy, like the Multipass Strategy, to use in attacking textbook chapters. Multipass has been found to be an effective strategy for students reading at or above the fourth grade level. Difficulties in demonstrating mastery of this strategy in grade level materials increase, however, as the gap between reading ability level and grade level widen, thus necessitating additional or different intervention procedures (Schumaker, Deshler, Alley, Warner, and Denton 1982).

Another widely recommended solution to the problem of LD students' reading assignments (Mosby 1980; Hartwell, Wiseman, and Van Reusen 1979) is the tape recording of textbook material. Persons who propose this procedure assume that tape-recorded reading assignments minimize students' reading deficits and allow them to stay current with class assignments by supplementing the information presented in classroom lectures. Taping content materials appears to be a viable alternative. Tape recorders, for example, are one of the most inexpensive and prevalent media devices. The National Needs Assessment of Educational Media and Materials for the Handicapped Report indicated that about 80 percent of classroom teachers have cassette recorders available to them (Vale 1980).

Although the tape recording of reading assignments is used frequently, the procedure has never been systematized, and the present way of tape-recording educational materials for secondary handicapped students suffers from the following shortcomings. First, LD teachers and other professionals usually do not have time for this time-consuming task. Consequently, parents, paraprofessionals, or normally achieving students often carry out the taping. Unfortunately, these individuals generally lack the necessary training and expertise for effective tape development. Second, most tape recordings do not follow known principles of learning and motivation. Instead, it is assumed that the verbatim transfer of reading materials is sufficient to overcome the student's reading problems. On the contrary, LD students often find materials that are taped verbatim to be boring, and thus may soon become unmotivated to learn content materials via this medium (Deshler and Graham 1980). Third, tapes which record printed material verbatim fail to take into account the unique characteristics and learning deficits of LD adolescents. Audio tapes for LD adolescents should be designed to compensate for the deficits evidenced by these students in information organization and manipulation, attention, memory, and listening and reading comprehension. Fourth, most tapings of educational materials do not provide sufficient opportunities for students to be *actively* involved in the learning process. Rather, students passively listen to the materials presented on the tapes. In short, traditional approaches to using tape-recorded materials for learning disabled adolescents as an alternative to printed materials have not met with much success. The primary reasons have been a failure to actively involve the student in the learning process and to design materials that incorporate known principles of learning and motivation to minimize the characteristics of the learning disabled adolescent.

The purpose of a project undertaken by the University of Kansas Institute for Research in Learning Disabilities was to design a set of procedures for effectively transferring content materials from a printed format to an audio format for LD adolescents who are unable to make use of the Multipass Strategy in their grade level materials. To overcome the numerous shortcomings in traditional audio-taping practices, the following guidelines proposed by Deshler and Graham (1980) were followed in the design of these audio tapes for LD adolescents: (1) taped materials were designed to include activities (such as having students regularly take notes and paraphrase key information) and techniques (such as advance organizers and summaries) that fostered text comprehension and motivation; (2) audio tapes were supplemented with other modified materials such as notetaking and outlining forms, study guides and key textbook markings; and (3) audio tapes were prepared so as to incorporate sound principles of learning such as repetition of key facts and concepts, use of corrective feedback, and active involvement of the learner at all phases of content acquisition and mastery.

Thus, each chapter in a textbook had a "package" of materials associated with it. The textbook chapter itself was marked using four colors of ink to cue key information. A study guide that specified key facts and concepts that should be learned accompanied each chapter. Also accompanying each chapter was an audio tape of the information in the chapter. Specific parts of the chapter (e.g., the introduction, topic sentences for main sections, the summary) were read verbatim, while other parts were paraphrased on the tape.

All material modification procedures were designed to be implemented by paraprofessionals. Paraprofessional involvement was considered to be crucial because of the limited time available to professional staff for major curriculum/material modification efforts. Paraprofessionals have been successfully employed in other special education assessment and instructional activities (Greer 1978; Goff and Kelly 1979; Boomer 1981), and thus were tapped as a major personnel resource for this project. A research project to show that paraprofessionals could produce the required modified materials which in turn could be used effectively by students was undertaken in addition to this current project (Deshler, Denton, and Schumaker 1982).

Finally, all procedures involved in this project took into consideration the notion that the educational needs of exceptional students are met when instructional materials are selected and/or modified to correspond with the handicapped students' unique attributes. The audiotaping procedure in this study was designed to meet that objective. In addition, however, it was also determined important to teach students appropriate strategies to effectively use these modified instructional materials and procedures. Thus, the purpose of this study was twofold: (1) to design procedures for modifying content reading assignments through the use of audio tapes, and (2) to teach LD adolescents a strategy for using the modified materials to improve their comprehension of grade-level textbook materials.

METHODOLOGY

Subjects

Sixteen secondary students (four junior high eighth graders and twelve senior high tenth graders) participated in this study. All were mainstreamed in social studies classes at their respective schools.

All four junior high students were classified as learning disabled and were trained to use the strategy. They attended two junior high schools and were enrolled in required American history classes in their schools. Of the twelve senior high students, six were classified as LD and were trained to use the strategy. The other six served in a comparison group; three of these students were classified as LD and three were considered to be low-achievers by their teachers. All twelve were enrolled in the same required basic world history class that was taught by a regular classroom teacher who cooperated in this study. No other students were enrolled in the class.

All the LD students in this study who were taught the strategy had IQs which measured in the low normal to above normal range, according to school records. The junior high students' WISC Full Scale IQ Scores ranged from 85 to 95 and the senior high students' ranged from 83 to 110 ($\overline{X}$ = 97). All of the LD students exhibited deficits in one or more achievement areas while not exhibiting physical or sensory handicaps, emotional disturbance, and economic, environmental, or cultural disadvantage. The reading comprehension grade level scores of the junior high LD students (as measured by the Stanford Diagnostic Test-Brown Level) ranged from 4.2 to 5.9 ($\overline{X}$ = 5.1) and of the senior high LD students who were taught the strategy ranged from 4.9 to 8.9 ($\overline{X}$ = 6.6). The auditory vocabulary grade level scores of the junior high LD students on the same test ranged from 5.3 to 7.2 ($\overline{X}$ = 6.2) and of the senior high LD students who were taught the strategy ranged from 7.5 to 11.9 ($\overline{X}$ = 9.98). The ages of the junior high LD students ranged from 14 years to 14 years 6 months ($\overline{X}$ = 14 yrs. 3 mos.). The senior high LD students' ages ranged from 15 yrs. 6 mos. to 17 yrs. ($\overline{X}$ = 16 yrs. 5 mos.).

The six high school students who served as the comparison group had full scale I.Q. scores that ranged from 85 to 112 ($\overline{X}$ = 98). Their reading comprehension grade level scores as measured by the Stanford Diagnostic Test (Brown level) ranged from 5.1 to 10.2 ($\overline{X}$ = 8.2), and their auditory vocabulary grade level scores as measured by the same test ranged from 7.2 to 11.9 ($\overline{X}$ = 9.9).* Their ages ranged from 15 years 7 mos. to 16 years 11 mos. ($\overline{X}$ = 16 yrs. 6 mos.).

The procedures of this study were explained to all the students and their parents and written consent was obtained.

Setting

The study took place in the classrooms of the three school sites (two junior high schools and one high school). All three schools were located in suburban, middle-class communities. Each student was seated at a desk or table in the learning center or library for the instruction.

Instructional Materials

The regular classroom textbook in use in each student's social studies class was adapted using the SOS taping procedure (Denton, Deshler, and

---

*The LD students in this group had reading grade level scores ranging from 5.1 to 6.4 ($\overline{X}$ = 5.3) and auditory vocabulary grade level scores ranging from 7.2 to 8.3 ($\overline{X}$ = 7.7).

Schumaker in preparation). This procedure includes the visually coded marking of key information in the chapter, and the preparation of a study guide over the key information. The two textbooks in use in the junior high schools (Bartlett, Keller, and Carey 1981; Wood and Gabriel 1971) had readability levels of 9.3 (samples ranged from 8.4 to 10.7) and 10.3 (samples ranged from 8.4 to 14.5), respectively. The one in use in the senior high school (Perry 1980) had an average readability level of 11.6 (samples ranged from 8.8 to 14.4). These textbooks were used in this study with the addition of visually cued markings on the pages. Therefore, each student was provided with a visually coded textbook, a tape recorder, a study guide for each chapter, and verbally cued tapes of chapters assigned in the regular classroom. These adaptations are hereafter referred to as chapter/tape material.

Procedures

The SOS strategy procedures

The SOS strategy was designed to include three sub-strategies: Survey, Obtain Information, and Self-test. Each of these substrategies required the student to use the chapter/tape materials in a particular way. The purpose of the Survey Substrategy is to familiarize the student with the main ideas and organization of the chapter. The chapter/tape contained information regarding the title of the chapter, the relationship of the current chapter to the chapter that preceded it and the chapter that followed it, the introduction to the chapter, the main ideas of the chapter, and the summary. During the Survey, the student was required to listen to the tape while following along in the visually coded text and to make a skeletal outline of the main headings in the chapter on an organizer worksheet. After the Student had listened to the Survey tape and completed the skeletal outline, the student paraphrased the information gained from the Survey. The students used an acronym (TRIMS) that stands for the five parts of the survey to help them remember the key information as they paraphrased it.

The purpose of the Obtaining Information Substrategy is for the student to obtain the most important facts and concepts from the chapter text. The importance of the information was judged by the regular classroom teachers who specified what information would be crucial for success on their classroom tests. The visually coded chapters and the tapes contained visual and verbal cues that helped the student know what information he/she was to place in his/her notes within the skeletal outline prepared during the Survey Substrategy. Thus, the Obtaining Information

Substrategy was designed to teach the student to attend to and take notes about the important information in the chapter. The desired result was that the student produce a set of notes on the chapter information that was complete and clear enough that the student could use the notes to review for a test over the key information from the text. After the student finished listening to the tape, he/she was required to review the chapter/tape and revise the notes until he/she could paraphrase all the information in his or her notes.

The purpose of the Self-Test Substrategy is for the student to do a self-check procedure that reveals what key information has been learned and what information still needs to be learned. For the Self-Test Substrategy, an indexing process was employed whereby the student used the study guide as a test. As the student asked him or herself about each item on the study guide, the student marked with a check the questions and items the student could answer or discuss without assistance. The student placed a box next to items that needed additional review, then the student referred to notes, the textbook and tape to find answers to boxed items on the study guide. After reviewing and learning the unknown items, the student then placed a checkmark in the boxes, indicating that the student felt the information had been learned satisfactorily. Once all the items had been checked, the student Self-Tested him or herself over all the items a final time.

Instructional procedures

Each student received individual training in the procedures from one of three instructors. Two of the instructors were certified LD teachers with an average of four years teaching experience in public school special education programs. The third instructor had no teaching experience. All three had Master's Degrees. The three instructors had been directly involved in the development of the procedures. The students met with their instructor for periods of time ranging from 30 to 50 minutes, three times a week during training. The students learned each substrategy to criterion in succession. Thus, they learned the Survey Substrategy to criterion before beginning to learn the Obtaining Information Substrategy, and they learned the Obtaining Information Substrategy to criterion before beginning to learn the Self-Test Substrategy.

The instructional procedures used to teach the substrategies were adapted for use from those outlined by Alley and Deshler (1979) and Deshler, Alley, Warner, and Schumaker (1980). Students progressed through the following instructional steps three times, once for each of the three substrategies.

Step 1: Test to Determine the Student's Current Learning Habit

In this step, the student's current mode of studying an assigned chapter from the regular classroom text was observed and analyzed. The student's score on the regular classroom test for the studied chapter was obtained. After testing was completed, the teacher discussed the results with the student, affirming that the student needed to improve his/her comprehension and retention of the information presented in the textbook chapter.

Step 2: Describe the Learning Strategy

Next, the teacher described the steps involved in the SOS substrategy and contrasted them with the student's current learning habit. The steps included the specific behaviors in which the student should engage and the sequence of behaviors which should be followed. As each step was explained, a rationale was given for why the behavior was important and how it would help the student to learn and remember the material more easily.

Step 3: Model the Strategy

In this step, the teacher modelled the substrategy for the student. Thus, the teacher demonstrated the substrategy by acting out each of the steps previously described to the student while "thinking aloud" so the student could witness all of the processes involved in the strategy.

Step 4: Verbal Rehearsal of the Strategy

Here, the student verbally rehearsed the steps involved in the substrategy to a criterion of 100 percent correct without prompts. This instructional step was designed to familiarize the student with the steps of the strategy such that he/she could instruct him/herself in the future as to what to do next when performing the substrategy.

Step 5: Practice with SOS Materials

In this instructional step, the student practiced applying the substrategy to successive chapters (or in the case of practice in the Obtaining Information Substrategy, to successive sections of a chapter). As the student became proficient in the strategy, he/she was encouraged to progress from overt self-instruction to covert self-instruction while practicing the strategy.

Step 6: Feedback

As the student applied the substrategy to a new chapter (or chapter section), the teacher gave the student both positive and corrective feedback. Steps 5 and 6 were recycled with additional chapters (or chapter sections) until the student learned to use the substrategy to a specified criterion.

Step 7: Test

The same test administered during Step 1 was given to the student again using a different textbook chapter. This test provided a measure of each student's progress in learning the substrategy. If the student met criterion on the test, instruction in the next substrategy was initiated. After the student met criterion on the last substrategy (Self-test), the student was instructed to use all three substrategies independently on chapters as they were assigned in class. If the student did not meet criterion on a mastery test, then Steps 5 and 6 were recycled until the student was ready for another mastery test.

Testing procedures and measurement

The students' chapter test scores were collected from the social studies teachers and used as an overall measure of effectiveness of the SOS strategy instruction and the modified materials. The chapter tests were those published in conjunction with the textbooks. The tests were administered under regular classroom conditions using typical testing procedures.

In addition to the regular classroom test scores, pre- and post-training measures were obtained that were related to the students' use of the SOS strategy. Two measures were related to each substrategy.

For the Survey Substrategy, the percentage of paraphrases made by the student that were related to the five parts of the Survey (Title, Relationship, Introduction, Main Ideas, and Summary) was determined (Subtest 1). Also, the students' skeletal outlines were analyzed to determine the percentage of items (consisting of the Title, Roman numerals, and main chapter headings) that were correctly inserted in the outline form (Subtest 2).

The two measures that were related to the Obtaining Information Substrategy were the percentage of information cued on the tape and in the textbook that the student had written into the outline (Subtest 1) and the percentage of cued information that the student could accurately paraphrase from his or her notes (Subtest 2). Thus, for both the Survey and Obtaining Information substrategies, the measures not only evaluated whether the students had written particular information in their notes but also whether they could explain what their notes meant.

The measures that were related to the Self-Test Substrategy included a measure of the percentage of Self-test steps appropriately followed by the student for all the items on the Study Guide (Subtest 1). They also included a measure of the percentage of questions/items on the study guide answered correctly (Subtest 2). These measures were obtained by directing the student to demonstrate how he/she would study for a test once a chapter assignment had been completed. While he or she studied, the student was directed to "think out loud." The instructor observed the student's study and review techniques and scored the behaviors on a specially prepared scoring sheet. All of the student's verbal responses that were related to his or her use of each of the substrategies were tape recorded.

Interobserver reliability was determined by having two instructors independently listen to the tapes or observe the student, and score the student's written products, once before and once after training for each measure for each student. The two scorers' results were compared item-by-item. An agreement was scored when both scorers recorded a particular behavior or response in exactly the same way. The percentage of agreement was calculated by dividing the number of agreements by the number of agreements plus disagreements and multiplying by 100. On the chapter tests, there were 626 agreements out of 632 opportunities to agree (99 percent agreement). On the Survey Subtest 1 there were 91 agreements out of 92 opportunities to agree (98.9 percent agreement); on the Survey Subtest 2 there were 59 agreements out of 64 opportunities to agree (92.1 percent agreement); on the Obtaining Information Subtest 1 there were 495 agreements out of 530 opportunities to agree (93.3 percent agreement); on the Obtaining Information Subtest 2 there were 99 agreements out of 105 opportunities to agree (94 percent agreement); on the Self-Test Subtest 1 there were 81 agreements out of 100 opportunities to agree (81 percent agreement); and on the Self-Test Subtest 2 there were 86 agreements out of 96 opportunities to agree (91 percent agreement).

Experimental Design

The multiple baseline design was employed in two ways. First, it was employed across substrategies for each of nine LD students to show the effects of the instructional methodology on the students' performance of the three parts of the SOS strategy. Thus, after the baseline condition where data on classroom tests and usage of the substrategies were collected, the three substrategies were taught separately, with the student reaching mastery on one substrategy before the subsequent substrategy was taught. Once the student had mastered all three substrategies, he/she performed the behaviors independently using the chapter/tapes for subsequently assigned chapters. The chapter/tape usage was timed to correspond with the regular classroom reading assignments such that the students were prepared to take the chapter tests when the tests were regularly scheduled for the class.

Additionally, the multiple baseline design was employed with six high school students to demonstrate the effects of three conditions on chapter test scores. The three conditions included: (1) the baseline condition, where students read the chapter as they normally did; (2) the verbatim tape condition, where students listened to a tape of someone reading the textbook chapter vertabim; and (3) the SOS condition where students used the SOS strategy and cued textbook and tapes. After achieving stability in the baseline condition, students received the verbatim condition together, and then received the SOS condition in a staggered sequence. Students 1, 2, and

3 received SOS training after four chapter tests. Students 2 and 4 received training after six chapter tests, and Student 6 received training after seven chapter tests. Six students in the same class served as a non-equivalent comparison group for the six LD students who received training. These comparison group students underwent baseline and verbatim tape conditions. They did not receive SOS training.

RESULTS

Multiple Baseline Results

Figures 9.1–9 show the results of the multiple baseline designs across substrategies for each of nine LD students. Figure 9.10 shows the results for a tenth LD student who did not receive the training within the same multiple baseline design format as the other students. All three substrategies were taught to her in two sessions to determine the feasibility of such training. Each figure consists of four graphs. The top three graphs show the data related to the two subtests for each of three substrategies in this order: the Survey data are in the top graph; the Obtaining Information data are in the second graph; and the Self-Test data are in the third graph. The fourth graph in each figure depicts the student's scores on chapter tests.

Figure 9.1 shows the results for one of the high school students, fictitiously named Matt. On chapter tests before the beginning of this study, Matt received scores ranging from 40 percent correct to 73 percent correct (shown by the squares). His teacher allowed him to retake all of the tests using his notes and the resulting test scores are depicted with dots. These scores ranged from 50 percent correct to 75 percent correct. On only two tests did Matt receive passing grades. After Matt listened to a verbatim tape of a textbook chapter, his score on the chapter test (shown with the star) was 40 percent correct.

Matt then began the "Instructional Baseline" condition where he was asked to independently survey the chapter, obtain information from the chapter, and study the chapter for a test. The two measures related to each of the substrategies were obtained three times to comprise this baseline condition for Matt. For survey, Matt noted and paraphrased less than 20 percent of the information required. After achieving stability on the Survey measures, Matt was instructed in the Survey Substrategy. He reached mastery in his second practice session (on the second chapter/tape presented to him) by noting and paraphrasing 100 percent of the required information. During baseline on obtaining information, Matt noted less than

Figure 9.1. The results of SOS Strategy training
for Student 1, a high school student.

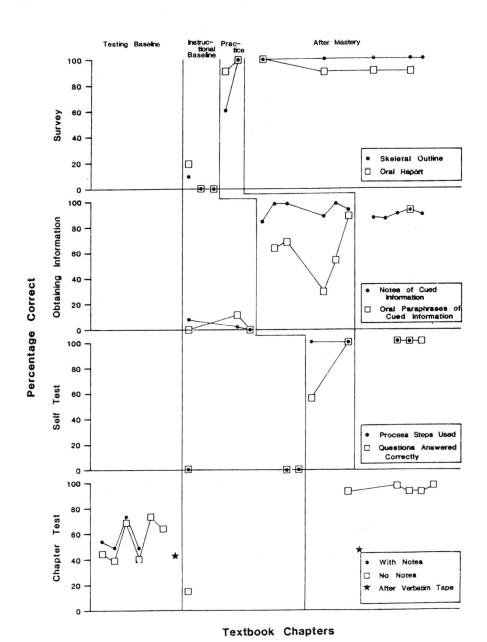

Figure 9.2. The results of SOS Strategy training
for Student 2, a high school student.

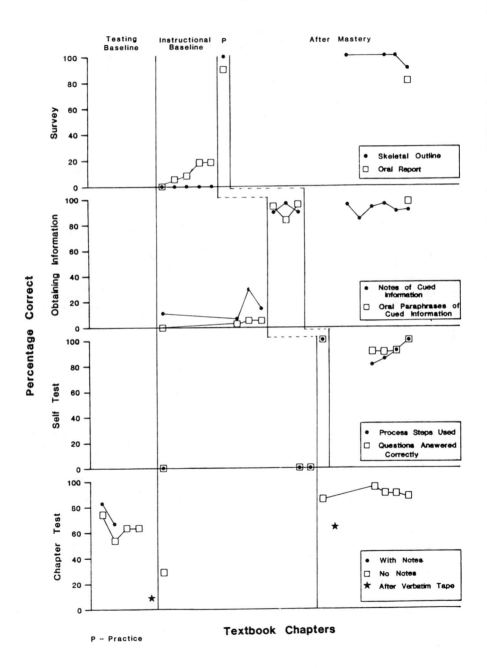

93

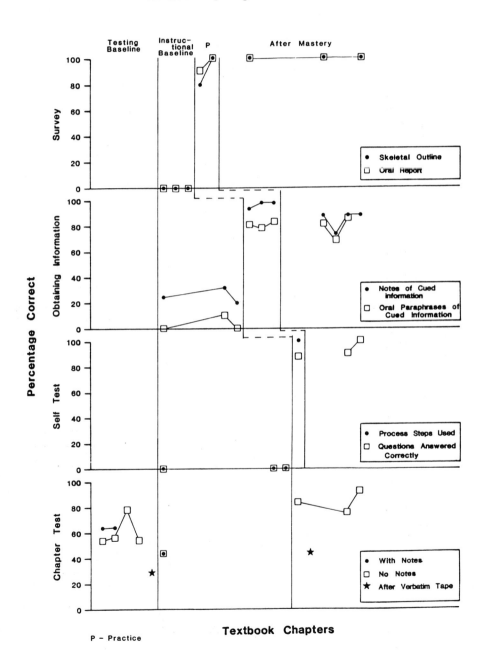

Figure 9.3. The results of SOS Strategy training for Student 3, a high school student.

Figure 9.4. The results of SOS Strategy training
for Student 4, a high school student.

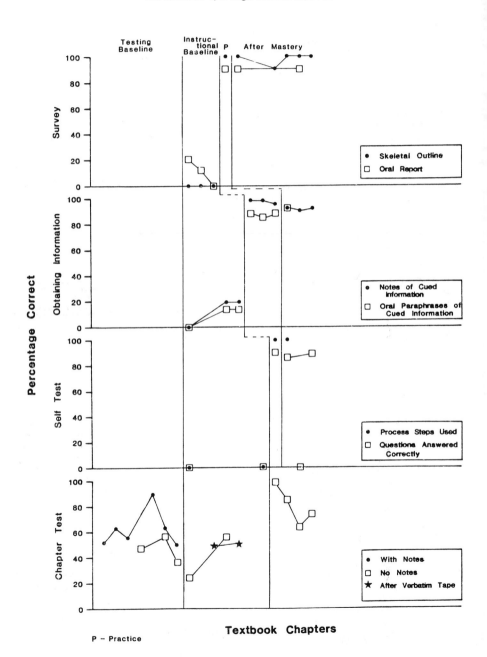

Figure 9.5. The results of SOS Strategy training for Student 5, a high school student.

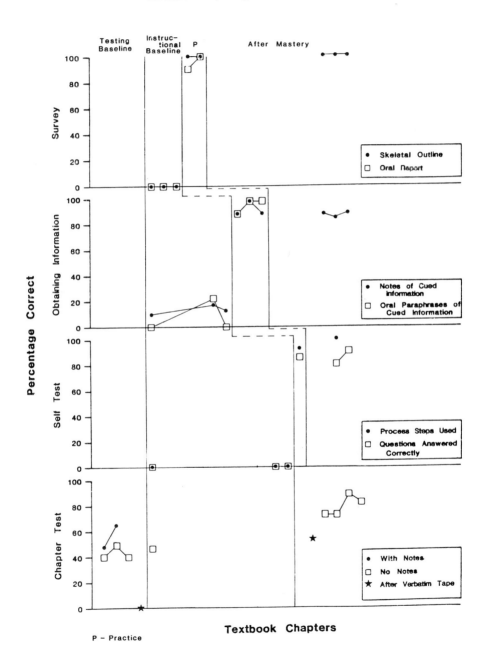

98

Figure 9.8. The results of SOS Strategy training
for Student 8, a junior high student.

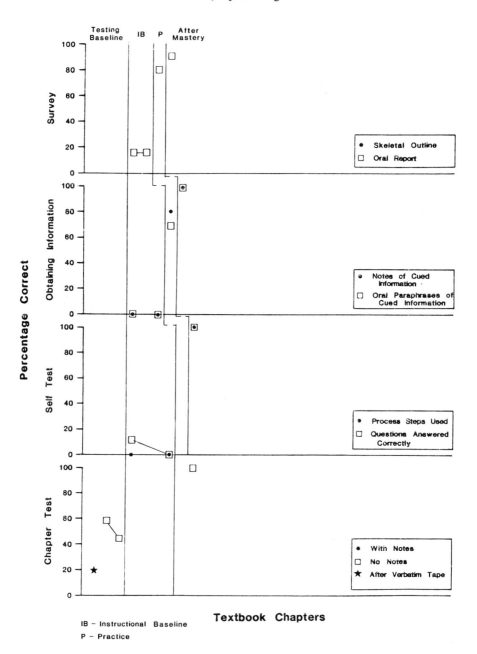

Textbook Chapters

IB – Instructional Baseline

P – Practice

Figure 9.9. The results of SOS Strategy training
for Student 9, a junior high student.

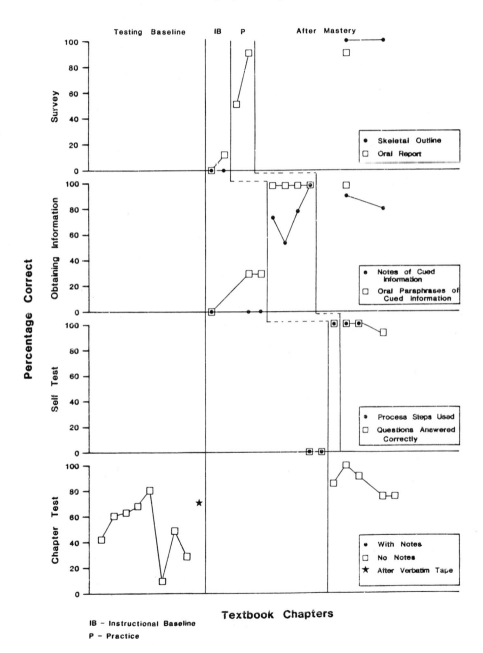

100

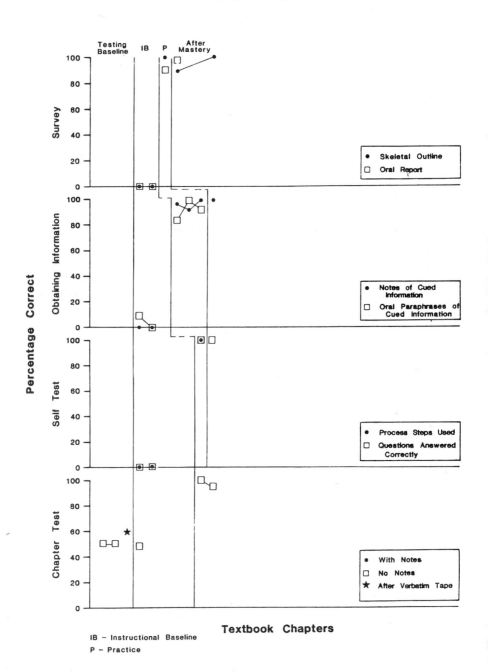

Figure 9.10. The results of SOS Strategy training for Student 10, a junior high student.

20 percent of the important information in the textbook and could paraphrase less than 10 percent of the important information. After training, he met mastery on obtaining information after using the procedures on the three sections of two chapters (a total of six sections). He was noting 95 percent of the required information and paraphrasing 90 percent of it correctly.

During baseline on the Self-Test measures, Matt did not use any of the Self-Test procedures, nor did he indicate that he knew any of the answers to questions on the study guide. After Self-Test training, Matt met mastery on the second chapter he processed by following all of the steps and answering all of the questions on the study guide.

After Matt had mastered the three parts of the SOS strategy, he was given the chapter tape, coded chapter, and study guide to use on his own each time the regular class teacher assigned a chapter. His notes and verbal responses were collected by the instructor whenever possible in addition to chapter test scores. Matt's test scores under these conditions ranged from 93 percent to 100 percent. He did not use his notes to complete these tests. When he was given a verbatim tape of a chapter during this condition, he received a score of 40 percent on the chapter test (shown by the star). Thus, Matt did not use the SOS strategies to criterion before he was trained on them, but he did after training. His use of the substrategies allowed him to remember more of the information and to perform at a highly acceptable level on the chapter tests in class.

Figures 9.2–10 show the results for the other students receiving SOS training. Figures 9.2–6 depict the results of senior high students and Figures 9.7–10 depict the results for the four junior high students. Figure 9.6 depicts the results for the student who received training on the SOS strategy in two, one-hour training sessions. She practiced the Survey Substrategy once, before being given instruction on the Obtaining Information Substrategy. She practiced this substrategy independently and then received Self-Test training. Thereafter, she used the strategy independently. The results from all the students are similar to Matt's. All of the students quickly mastered the strategy and showed markedly improved performances on the chapter tests. These improvements only took place after instruction was implemented in each case.

Figure 9.11 shows the results from the multiple baseline across students design. Depicted are the chapter test scores for each student. The results show that the chapter test scores for the students improved only after the students received SOS training. They did not improve after the students had listened to verbatim tapes (depicted with the squares). The average test score of the high school LD students who received SOS training in the Baseline Condition was 55 percent, in the Verbatim tape condition was 41 percent, and in the SOS condition was 89 percent.

102

Figure 9.11. The percentage correct on chapter tests
for LD high school students before and after learning the SOS Strategy.

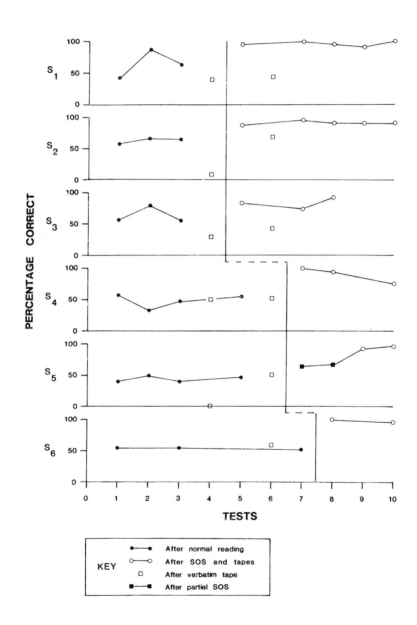

Table 9.1 shows the results of the comparison between the LD students who received SOS training and the students who did not receive training. As can be seen from the data, the students who did not receive the training did not improve over the course of the school semester. Their average test score in the normal reading condition was 56 percent which was comparable to the baseline failing scores of the students who did receive training. These students also showed no improvement when they listened to the verbatim tape before the chapter tests (on chapters 16 and 21). The average test score for these students was 51 percent in the Verbatim Tape Condition.

Instructional Time

The time involved in teaching the three substrategies was as follows. To present the Survey Substrategy (Steps 2–4) required 15 minutes of teacher time. Each practice trial (Steps 5 and 6) required 10 minutes. To present the Obtaining Information substrategy took 45 minutes and each practice trial required 30 minutes. Finally, the Self-Test Substrategy required 10 minutes to present and 30 minutes for each practice trial. With Student 6, this time was shortened by presenting all of the Survey and Obtaining Information instruction in one class period. The student practiced the Survey Substrategy once in this session. Then student practiced both substrategies for homework that night. Then the assignment was reviewed and the student was instructed in the Self-Test Substrategy in a second class period the next day. Thus, as long as the student does not require repeated practice to master a substrategy, instruction in SOS can be accomplished in as few as two class periods.

DISCUSSION

The results of this study support the conclusion that LD adolescents can be taught to apply a complex learning strategy to modified materials to facilitate their comprehension of information from grade level textbooks. The application of this strategy to these modified materials resulted in LD students receiving passing grades on chapter tests administered under normal conditions in the regular classroom that were markedly higher than pretraining test scores. LD students who had been failing regular classroom chapter tests began to excel over students who took the same tests but did not use the SOS strategy and materials. All of the students who were taught

Table 9.1
Effects of SOS Taping Strategy with High School Students
on *Unfinished Journey* Tests

Students	Chapter 12	Chapter 13	Semester Exam	AVT‡ Chap. 16	Chapter 20	AVT‡ Chap. 21	Chapter 22	Chapter 25	Chapter 26	Chapter 27	Average Exam Score w/o SOS	Average Exam Score with SOS & Tape
SOS GROUP												
1	42	75	63	40	96*	44	100*	96*	92*	100*	55	97
2	58	67	66	10	88*	68	96*	92*	92*	92*	54	92
3	58	80	57	30	84*	44	76*	92*	—	—	54	84
4	58	33	48	50	56	52	100*	84*	—	76*	49	87
5	40	50	40	0	48	52	64†	68†	92*	84*	44	88
6	54	—	54	—	—	60	52	100*	—	96*	55	98
CONTROL GROUP												
7	62	—	56	—	69	40	48	64	32	64	54	
8	54	73	—	—	56	60	36	36	48	52	52	
9	77	47	56	60	44	64	36	48	72	78	58	
10	46	67	62	10	60	64	56	48	—	—	52	
11	62	93	—	—	56	56	76	84	64	78	71	
12	—	33	—	—	32	56	20	—	—	—	35	

*Student applied SOS Strategy using chapter and audio-tapes.
†Student used the audio-tape but did not self-test.
‡After verbatim tape.

SOS recognized the fact that the strategy was beneficial to use in their history reading assignments; members of the class who were not taught SOS expressed dissatisfaction that they had not been allowed to learn the strategy and use the modified materials.

The successful results of the SOS strategy and materials with regard to textbook comprehension are a marked contrast from the test scores resulting from the use of verbatim tapes. This finding is particularly significant because of the heavy reliance by special educators on verbatim taping of textbook materials as a material modification procedure. The SOS results underscore the importance of incorporating sound learning principles into material modifications and of not assuming that the student can automatically benefit from material modifications by changing the format or mode of instructional delivery alone. In short, these findings suggest that students who have difficulty handling written materials may also have difficulty dealing with auditory materials as well. One key to improving comprehension through audio tapes is to teach the student a specific strategy for dealing with the newly formulated materials.

Perhaps the major implication of these results is the fact that this procedure represents a means by which the learning disabled student can independently keep abreast of the large numbers and volume of reading assignments given to secondary students. In turn, the need for tutorial assistance in content areas is reduced and the resource room teacher can devote the majority of his/her time to instructing students in deficient skills or strategies.

Some cautionary statements or possible limitations should be noted when considering these promising results. First, while the procedure has been streamlined as much as possible and designed with public school applications in mind, it still requires a certain amount of personnel, materials, and equipment coordination to insure its success. Second, classroom textbooks are revised and/or changed every few years. To avoid wasting the efforts and time put into marking and taping a given text it is important to insure that the text will be used in a given district for several years to come. Third, the importance of insuring the motivation of the student in the use of the SOS strategy in the modified materials is central to its continued use. The support of both the content and resource teacher in this regard is very important.

Finally, there are several questions remaining to be answered. Among them are the following: (1) Can students achieve comparable results by using the SOS strategy with a marked text alone (without the audio tape)? (2) Can the SOS procedure be applied with equal success to other subject areas (e.g., science, mathematics, vocational education)? And (3) to what degree must the SOS procedure be modified to accommodate LD adolescents with minimal reading skills? These questions will be addressed by our Institute as we continue to refine the SOS procedure.

REFERENCES

Alley, G., and D. Deshler. *Teaching the Learning Disabled Adolescent: Strategies and Methods.* Denver: Love, 1979.

Bartlett, R. A., C. W. Keller, and H. H. Carey. *Freedom's Trail.* Boston: Houghton Mifflin, 1981.

Boomer, L. W. "Meeting Common Goals through Effective Teacher-Paraprofessional Communication." *Teaching Exceptional Children* 13 (1981): 51–53.

Brandis, M., and R. Halliwell. *Verification of Procedures to Serve Handicapped Students: Final Report—Secondary Component* (Contract No.: 300-79-0702). Silver Springs, Md.: Applied Management Sciences, 1980.

Carlson, S. "Descriptive Summary of Students Served in Child Service Demonstration Centers." In D. Wisemen, ed., *Issues and Practices in Secondary Learning Disabilities* Tempe: Arizona State University Press, 1979.

Denton, P. H., D. D. Deshler, and J. B. Schumaker. *Instructional Manual for the SOS Taping Procedures* (Research Monograph No. 16). Lawrence, Kans.: University of Kansas Institute for Research in Learning Disabilities, in preparation.

Deshler, D. D., G. R. Alley, M. M. Warner, and J. B. Schumaker. Instructional Practices for Promoting Skill Acquisition and Generalization in Severely Learning Disabled Adolescents. *Learning Disability Quarterly* 4 (1981): 415–421.

Deshler, D. D., P. H. Denton, and J. B. Schumaker. *Training Paraprofessionals to Produce Integrated Curriculum Modifications* (Research Report No. 70). Lawrence, Kans. University of Kansas Institute for Research in Learning Disabilities, in preparation.

Deshler, D. D., and S. Graham. "Tape Recording Educational Materials for Secondary Handicapped Students." *Teaching Exceptional Children* 12 (1980): 52–54.

Deshler, D. D., N. Lowrey, and G. R. Alley. "Programming Alternatives for LD Adolescents: A Nationwide Survey." *Academic Therapy* 14 (1979): 389–397.

Greer, J. U. "Utilizing Paraprofessionals and Volunteers in Special Education." *Focus on Exceptional Children* 10 (1978): 1–15.

Goff, M., and P. Kelly. "The Special Education Paraprofessional and the Individualized Education Program Process." *Focus on Exceptional Children* 10 (1979): 10–13.

Hartwell, L. K., D. E. Wiseman, and A. Van Reusen. "Modifying Course Content for Mildly Handicapped Students at the Secondary Level." *Teaching Exceptional Children* 12, no. 1 (1979): 28–32.

Moran, M. R. *An Investigation of the Demands on Oral Language Skills of Learning Disabled Students in Secondary Classrooms* (Research Report No. 1). Lawrence: The University of Kansas Institute for Research in Learning Disabilities, 1980.

Mosby, R. "The Application of the Developmental By-pass Procedure to LD Adolescents." *Journal of Learning Disabilities* 13, no. 7 (1980): 21–27.

Perry, M. *Unfinished Journey: A World History.* Boston: Houghton Mifflin, 1980.

Schumaker, J. B., D. D. Deshler, G. R. Alley, M. M. Warner, and P. H. Denton. "Multipass: A Learning Strategy for Improving Reading Comprehension." *Learning Disability Quarterly* 5 (1982): 295–304.

Vale, C. A. *National Needs Assessment of Educational Media and Materials for the Handicapped.* Berkeley, Cal.: Educational Testing Service, 1980.

Warner, M. M., J. B. Schumaker, G. R. Alley, and D. D. Deshler. "Learning Disabled Adolescents in the Public Schools: Are They Different from Other Low Achievers?" *Exceptional Education Quarterly* 1 (1980): 27–36.

Wiederholt, L., and B. McEntire. "Educational Options for Handicapped Adolescents." *Exceptional Education Quarterly* 1, no. 2 (1980): 1–11.

Wood, L. C., and R. H. Gabriel. *America: Its People and Values.* New York: Harcourt Brace Jovanovich, 1971.

10

Group Screening for Language Learning Disabilities in Junior High, High School, and Community College Populations

Jacquelyn Gillespie

FEDERAL LEGISLATION requiring school districts to provide appropriate instruction for all handicapped students has also, under "search-and-serve" provisions, mandated the identification of students in need of special instructional services. Especially in districts where the mobility rate is high and schools must accommodate a high proportion of new students each year, many with only sketchy records of previous school progress, the problem of identifying students with learning disabilities assumes major proportions. The situation is especially difficult in junior and senior high schools, since in those settings no one teacher provides the close teacher contact and follow-up available to elementary school students. Community colleges are also increasingly aware of learning problems in their populations, with specialized reading instruction and learning disability programs often available to help otherwise competent students manage the reading and composition demands of the college program.

The establishment of an individual learning disability requires careful individual assessment. However, it is also of primary importance to identify students in need of individual assessment procedures. Most schools rely on the individual referral process, which requires an observant teacher or well-informed parent to initiate action on the student's behalf. Group achievement test scores are sometimes available, but often they are neither current nor readily available to the classroom teacher, who is the vital link in the initial identification process.

The following structure, used as an initial orientation procedure in English classes, can be used to obtain not only the usual information that teachers find routinely useful but also to flag for observation students who give indications of special instructional needs. The procedures are deceptively simple but require certain basic applications of psychological observation techniques to bring teachers into the assessment process effectively.

1. The classroom teacher should obtain information on a teacher-made

form from each student, to include name, address, and phone number, and current schedule of classes, including names of teachers. Students who have difficulty with this apparently simple task, including those who avoid completing it, are giving indication of some sort of initial difficulty making adjustments to their new schedule.

There are several possibilities that may contribute to problems in completing the information requested on the form:

The student simply may not know the information. However, this fact in itself would be a major indication of difficulty in a student of junior high school age or older. On the first day of school, for a student new to the school, some confusion may be understandable. By the end of the first week of school, continuing inability to describe the daily routine is not typical. Correct spelling of unusual teacher names will, of course, continue to be a problem for many students, particularly at junior high school level. However, students with facility in spelling will have the names spelled correctly and will probably handle all other routine tasks in written expression well, at least at a rote level. Note that the issue here is ROTE and ROUTINE, since that level of information is all that is required for the correct completion of the assigned task. The ability to complete the task successfully suggests good awareness of time and place, the ability to organize and give back the information on request and in the form in which the information was requested. It also implies that the student is therefore at least minimally socially aware of the structure of the school environment and is able to organize data at a basic level.

The student who has difficulty with the task may have basic deficits in cognitive understanding of the school setting and/or the nature of the task; problems of this kind would not be unexpected in a student with some mental retardation.

The student may alternatively have a disorder in perception of time sequence.

The student may have any of several varieties of memory disturbance.

A dysgraphic language disorder may also inhibit the ability to put down in the required form information that the student can provide orally.

Perhaps serious anxiety about the school or some aspect of it may inhibit the ability to focus on its structure or generally interfere with logical reasoning processes.

Other types of emotional disorder which interfere with the orderly processing of information may also result in an inability to cope with the task.

The student who refuses the task or avoids it in some fashion may be aware of difficulty in completing the task and may use avoidance to keep others from identifying the problem. Many students go to extraordinary lengths to keep others from noting their weaknesses.

Some of the possible alternatives can be eliminated by careful questioning of the student. Others may require individual assessment by specialists.

2. The classroom teacher should ask the students to write two brief paragraphs to assess composition skills — one on what was best about the previous school year, and one on what was worst. This kind of assignment not only identifies composition strengths and weaknesses but, through the choice of topic, gives an idea about the student's fears and hopes for the current year, which have direct bearing on motivation and classroom success. Reasonable success with this task suggests that the student has a fundamental grasp of composition as a particular kind of communicative activity. It says nothing about the student's ability to comprehend various kinds of subject matter beyond his or her own personal experience.

The breadth and depth of a student's school experience and life experience, as well as cognitive flexibility and cultural background, are all important issues in the ability to handle the content demands of a particular course of instruction. However, it is important to separate those variables from those which are specifically related to learning disabilities.

Indications of major disorders in the ability to handle written language are usually most readily discernible in composition assignments of all sorts. It is particularly important that a student's initial efforts to complete a written assignment be given careful scrutiny. Carelessness should never be simply accepted as a reason for poor performance; reasons for the carelessness should be established. If an assignment is repeated with marked improvement, then the original carelessness marks an attitude problem that may predict continuing problems in the classroom. More often, repetition does not produce improvement.

It is well to keep in mind that many students with learning disorders do not know that they have specific learning difficulties. They have been told repeatedly that they are careless, and they have come to believe that explanation for their scholastic problems. Careful observation identifies quite readily the student who is actually able to do fine work with adequate incentives and controls and the one whose most intense efforts produce hopelessly inadequate responses.

The automatic aspects of composition, like the automatic aspects of reading, are usually performed consistently in well established habit patterns — rather like tying shoelaces. The student at junior high level or above who must be reminded to use capital letters and punctuation, to write in complete sentences, and to use some sort of logical ordering principle in writing is either woefully lacking in instruction or attempting to cope with a form of disability in written expression. The basic elements of capital letters, punctuation, etc., are usually learned simply from observation of the organization of any printed page in a book or newspaper. The need for formal instruction in these areas is seldom necessary beyond grades four or five. It is the student who is obviously bright and verbal who tends to suffer most from having dyslexic and/or dysgraphic disabilities ignored or punished, since assumptions are often made that oral fluency, good vocabulary, and good reasoning ability are automatically reflected in strong writing capability.

The inability to write at a minimally effective level is probably the most common area of inadequacy afflicting students from grades seven and up. Nevertheless, the existence of an actual disability in the area of written expression is often ignored in situations where a good deal of attention is given to the identification of reading problems.

Reading and writing are two aspects of the same process — reading is an input activity and writing is an output activity, both using the secondary symbol system of written symbols to stand for oral language. Writing requires complex recall and productive abilities that are not necessary in reading, where the stimulus material is provided. Therefore, individuals who are competent readers are not always competent in writing ability. However, someone who is capable of writing effectively is nearly always at least equally competent in reading, since the receptive capabilities are precursors of the abilities necessary for written expression. A measure of written expression, then, is the first and easiest way to identify those who may be expected to function effectively in the basic areas of reading and writing. Identification of students with adequate composition skills frees the teacher to concentrate, for assessment purposes, on those students who exhibit deficits in one or more aspects of skills development.

Problems in written expression, like those in reading, may derive from a variety of sources and require careful assessment. However, the identification of an actual language learning disability may be facilitated through assessment of coding efficiency, or the ability to move easily and automatically from the sounds and structure of the spoken word to the patterns and structure of the written word. Coding efficiency underlies the effective use of the secondary symbol system of language in print. The inability to manage the automatic coding processes is a basic indication of a true language learning disability.

3. It is possible to measure individual coding effectiveness in a group situation with the use of the Diagnostic Analysis of Reading Errors (DARE). This instrument uses a multiple-choice spelling test format to identify the ability of individuals to associate words as they are heard with words as they are written. Incorrect responses provide measures of certain kinds of responses typically made by learning disabled individuals but not by those in the general population. The test can be machine or hand scored. It is practical, therefore, to administer the test to an entire classroom of students, or to identify the individuals who perform poorly on the writing

samples described earlier and give them the test in a small group. It is also feasible to give the simple assessment procedures to several classes and pull from those classes the students who exhibit difficulty for further screening with the DARE.

The Correct score on the DARE provides an overall measure of coding efficiency and a standardized indication of whether or not a student meets mastery criteria. The test also provides error scores that indicate the nature of coding problems demonstrated by each individual. Error responses reflect difficulties with word structure (Omission errors), sequencing (Reversal errors), or English language sounds (Sound Substitution errors). Test scores, then, provide not only a gross indication of coding skills but also describe the nature of any coding deficits.

Those students who have problems with the kinds of rote associative language processes measured by the DARE may then be given further assessment as appropriate. For example, the Wide Range Achievement Test (WRAT) may be used in both reading and spelling to provide a comparative measure of expressive language coding skills. The WRAT is used routinely in many school districts as part of the learning disability identification process.

The combination of a writing sample and the DARE results have been used in a writing project at Indiana Vocational and Technical College in Indianapolis. According to Mary Lou Montgomery and Lee Churchill, the predicted end-of-course grades in composition derived from DARE scores were more accurate than those predicted by the original writing sample, suggesting the importance of the coding process in the development of writing skills.

The use of writing samples plus the DARE can vastly simplify screening for language learning disabilities. The procedure provides a relatively time- and cost-efficient way of surveying English classes at the beginning of the school year to identify the various levels of basic language effectiveness in the classroom related to coding proficiency. With the occasional consultation help of a psychologist, relatively simple assessment procedures can give the teacher a wealth of information for instructional planning, as well as provide preliminary screening information concerning individuals who may need further assessment for possible language learning disabilities.

REFERENCE

Gillespie, J., and Shohet, J. *Diagnostic Analysis of Reading Errors.* Wilmington, Del.: Jastak, 1979.

STEPS TO EMPLOYMENT

11

Seven Steps to Employment
for Learning Disabled Students

Lloyd W. Tindall

For too long a period of time learning disabled people have been underrepresented in vocational education and job training programs in the United States. Learning disabled persons have not shared equally in vocational education programs, workstudy, apprenticeship or in job training. This situation has resulted in higher unemployment, underemployment and in lower wages for the learning disabled population. White, Schumaker, Warner, Alley, and Deshler (1980) in a study of LD young adults found that they had lower level jobs and were significantly less satisfied with their employment than were their non-LD peers. Existing vocational education curricula and programs to be developed under the new Job Training and Partnership Act (JTPA) can be valuable avenues to employment for learning disabled persons. Computer assisted instruction is opening up a whole new world of learning potential for the learning disabled student.

Research directed at the needs of learning disabled adolescents and adults has been extremely fruitful during the last five years. The Institute for Research in Learning Disabilities at the University of Kansas has conducted extensive studies with emphasis on Adolescents and Young Adults (Clark 1981). Deshler, Schumaker, Alley, Warner, and Clark (1982) have provided research implications of these studies. Vocational and career assessment for learning disabled students is now at a very usable stage. Brown (1982), Grisafe (1983), and others have laid out viable vocational and career assessment programs for learning disabled and other handicapped students. The potential to assist learning disabled persons to obtain employment and establish meaningful careers has never been more promising. However, the problem which still remains is how to utilize the current research and previously known information in a manner which benefits teachers and learning disabled students. This presentation attempts to outline the concepts of a program designed to assist special and vocational education teachers, parents and others in the development of appropriate vocational and job training programs for learning disabled students. The seven step approach will emphasize the process, teaching methods and modifications which are necessary and which can be applied to current vocational and job training programs.

These steps are interwoven and will necessarily be carried out simultaneously. After the listing of the seven steps, each step will be discussed in detail.

Step One: Assessment and Evaluation
Step Two: Provide Support Services
Step Three: Develop Interagency Linkages
Step Four: Provide Help to Vocational and Other Educators
Step Five: Provide Skill Development for Learning Disabled Students
Step Six: Provide Placement Services
Step Seven: Plan for Lifetime Education

STEP ONE: ASSESSMENT AND EVALUATION

An appropriate assessment and evaluation of learning disabled students can help teachers prepare meaningful Individualized Education Programs for learning disabled students and to develop appropriate curricula and support services. Vocational and career assessment can assist the learning disabled student in determining their interests and abilities as they relate to the world of work. Brown stated that profile scatter on tests like the WISC-R may range from retarded to genius across skills. Behaviors may range from passive helplessness to angry, aggressive acting out to pleasantly appropriate. A learning disabled person's careers and expectations may range from none to professional levels. Learning disabled students are a heterogeneous group and no single test battery can provide the answers to the questions asked by the evaluators.

Hooper (1980) speculated that most workers are fired, not because of their lack of skill or ability to do the job, but due to the inability to deal with authority, get along with others or to acquire socially acceptable skills. LD persons frequently fail to perceive social situations accurately, identify appropriate models, or pick up subtle social clues and non-verbal communications (Cook 1979). Such behavior often is exhibited on the job and results in serious problems for the LD person. Other authors have addressed the vocational assessment of learning disabled as well as non-LD students, McCray (1982); Kapes and Mastie (1982); Vacc and Bardon (1982). A timely and important manual on vocational assessment of students with special needs was published by the East Texas State University Occupational Curriculum Lab (1982).

The point here is that LD students possess a great many problems which act as barriers to education and employment. Current evaluation instruments and techniques can identify these situations and provide some answers.

Evaluation Goals and Student Orientation

The goals of the assessment need to be defined prior to the beginning of the assessment process. Is the goal to assist in IEP development, determine cognitive ability, interest, aptitudes, skills, or other areas of concern for the LD student, and his or her teachers and parents? The LD student and parents if appropriate need orientation as to the assessment goals, how the assessments will be carried out, how assessments will be scored and interpreted and how results will be used and by whom. You may also want to provide for oral testing and taping the students feedback. Finally, a decision must be made on who will administer the instruments.

The following educational, psychological and vocational evaluation instruments were selected to provide the reader with an idea of the type of materials which might be used to assess an LD student. There are scores of other instruments available. The time elapsed from the first educational and psychological tests to vocational evaluations may cover a several year span or a few months span. The following instruments have been successfully used in assessing both adolescents and adults with learning problems.

Educational and Psychological Evaluations

Evaluators are faced with an enormous number of instruments from which to choose. It is suggested that the reader become familiar with the writings of the previously listed authors and others when conducting evaluations. Persons charged with the evaluation of learning disabled students may be interested in some tests which are commonly used. Dr. Michael Trevitt at Santa Ana College develops an assessment summary from three tests and then makes a decision as to whether more tests are required. These tests are (1) Wechsler Adult Intelligence Scale — Revised (WAIS-R); (2) Bender Motor Gestalt; and (3) The Peabody Individual Achievement Test (PIAT). The WAIS-R measures the intellectual functioning and can be used for a diagnosis of handicap and for placement decisions. The Bender Motor Gestalt is used to identify an organic impairment such as brain damage. The PIAT is designed to survey the level of educational attainment in basic skills and knowledge and can be used in diagnosis of handicap and in

evaluation of progress and placement decisions. In addition to these instruments Pfieffer (1983) would add the Purdue Perceptual Motor Survey
to identify occular motor problems, the Keystone Telebinocular and subsequent cards to identify a visual perceptual learning disability, the Illinois
Test of Psycholinguistic Abilities to measure visual and auditory reception
and association and verbal and manual expression. Pfieffer also recommended the visual perception and motor response parts of the Slingerland
Screening Tests.

Another popular and widely used test, the Wechsler Intelligence Scale
for Children — Revised (WISC-R), is designed to assess the person's capacity to understand and cope with the world. The WISC-R will also help
in IEP development by indicating developmental deficiencies which require
remediation. Finally the Woodcock, Johnson Psychoeducational Battery
(WJPB) may be given to provide a measurement of reading, written language, and math.

Vocational Evaluations

Vocational evaluations can be used to assess vocational interests and
abilities. According to Grisafe it is best to assess vocational interests before vocational abilities. This will maximize a students occupational exploration before considering the limiting factor of abilities. Sharing the
results of an interest inventory with the learning disabled student will expand the number and diversity of occupations that he or she will want
to investigate. Although there are many interest tests, six popular tests suitable for learning disabled students are the (1) California Occupational Preference System (COPS). COPS is designed for senior high and college and
provides a systematic measurement of students' interests and strengths in
clusters of meaningful related occupations; (2) COPS II Intermediate is
a similar instrument designed for elementary grade students or higher grade
students; (3) The Ohio Vocational Interest Survey (OVIS) is useful for adolescents and surveys the students' interest in the world of work; (4) Strong
Campbell Interest Inventory for higher level occupations; (5) the Department of Labor's Interest Inventory; and (6) the Wide Range Interest Opinion Test (WRIOT) for non-readers.

Common instruments for assessing abilities and skills are (1) Talent
Assessment Program (TAP). TAP measures the individual skills in dexter-
ity and discrimination tasks that the developer has determined to be related to clusters of jobs; (2) Career Ability Placement Survey (CAPS).
CAPS results are summarized in the form of a normed graph which matches

the student's abilities to fourteen occupational category scales. CAPS has a fourth grade reading level; and (3) the Program for Assessing Youth Employment Skills (PAYES). PAYES uses a combination of pictures and related questions which are read to the assessee. PAYES assesses work attitudes and cognitive development in relation to occupations and vocational interest.

Work sample evaluation systems are used to evaluate work potential. Three work sample tests which are widely used are mentioned here. Many other commercially developed work samples are available along with hundreds of homemade work samples which are usually developed by local evaluators utilizing local shop and laboratory equipment. The Jewish Employment and Vocational Services (JEVS) produces a work sample system for disabled adolescents and adults which assesses interests, behavior and performance relating to work capabilities. Valpar Corporation builds work samples for use with handicapped students which measures traits related to a person's success in occupations across a number of job families. Singer has built work oriented screening devices designed to help students make vocational choices.

Giving and Interpreting the Assessment Instruments

All of the above-mentioned evaluation instruments are used on various populations. They are not specifically designed for learning disabled students. This may mean that tests will have to be given orally which may interfere with the established norms. The list is not an all inclusive, hundreds of other instruments are available. The instruments should not be used in isolation. They measure only a situation at a given place and time. The instruments provide one kind of information. Teachers, psychologists, employers and parents can provide another kind of information. A dialogue session of the persons given the tests needs to be convened to discuss the results and provide appropriate interpretations. Interpretations is the most important part of the assessment process and the student is the most important person with whom to share the interpretation (Grisafe 1983). The assessment results need to be communicated to special and vocational educators, job training personnel and parents and others as appropriate in the development of the IEP, modified vocational and job training programs or work study, apprenticeship training, and job placement. The assessment is not an end in itself but a tool to help meet predetermined goals. An appropriate assessment is a real asset to the LD student and to those who will be providing him or her education and training services.

STEP TWO: PROVIDING SUPPORT SERVICE

Supportive services coordinated to provide assistance to the learning disabled student are a must. Similar services need to be provided to both secondary and postsecondary LD students. Supportive services include tutoring, evaluation, counseling, notetaking, tape recorders, testing assistance, textbook study helps, job seeking and job placement helps, talking books and adapted P.E. Other services such as registration assistance, financial aid and campus orientation may need to be provided by postsecondary supportive service units.

Whether at the secondary or postsecondary level, learning disabled students need someone in an advocacy role. This advocate must serve as a bridge between the vocational teachers and the special education teachers. At the postsecondary level the bridge is between the LD student and the vocational teachers. Perhaps a strong supportive role will be played without direct contact with the vocational teachers.

The person filling the advocate role could be from various school based backgrounds such as a learning disabilities coordinator, special education teacher or special needs coordinator. At least two states provide programs which provide a full time position designed to help handicapped students enter and function effectively in the vocational classroom and laboratory. These are the Designated Vocational Instructor Program in Wisconsin and the Related Vocational Instructor Program in Georgia. Whatever the title of the advocate, the position needs to be full time and provide the following services.

1. Provide a link between special education and vocational education and work with the LD student to function effectively in the vocational classroom.
2. Coordinate school and community resources.
3. Promote teacher-student relationships.
4. Provide support to vocational teachers in techniques and strategies for teaching LD students.
5. Deal with the LD students daily problems.
6. Facilitate the utilization of alternative tests and materials

STEP THREE: DEVELOP INTERAGENCY LINKAGES

Providing the necessary services to help LD students enroll in and function effectively in vocational education and training programs and to achieve job placement and become established in meaningful careers will require the help and cooperation of personnel within the school system and the assistance of various community agencies. Although the person in the advocate position fulfills a vital role there remains a need to further expand the task of providing services to the LD student. Interagency linkage is a tool to be used in gaining the coordination and assistance of others in the community. Vocational rehabilitation counselors have services of value to the LD student. Coordination of the IEP and the Individualized Written Rehabilitation Programs needs to be made where appropriate. Other agencies, employers and businesses have services to offer. The new Job Training and Partnership Act (JTPA) has a 1983–1984 budget of 3.8 billion dollars. Forty percent of the monies must be spent on youth aged 16–21. Ninety percent of the recipients of services must be economically disadvantaged. Many LD persons are in this category. Ten percent of the monies must be spent on specific categorical groups such as handicapped students. This ten percent would be 380 million nationally. Eight percent of the monies are for state education and training grants. The Governors of each state are given the responsibility to distribute these funds. The Private Industry Councils (PIC) within the Service Delivery Areas (SDA) and the State Education Agencies receiving the eight percent funds will be developing JTPA programs. The JTPA identifies 28 uses of fund categories. Some of these categories suitable for LD students are (1) job search assistance; (2) job counseling; (3) remedial education and basic skills training; (4) on the job training; (5) education-to-work transition activities; (6) work experience; (7) vocational exploration; (8) job development; and (9) institutional skill training.

The needs of learning disabled students need to be made known to the PICs. At least 51 percent of the PICs must be made up of persons from the private sector, thus linkages to the PICs is a vital interagency linkage. It may also be possible under certain conditions for secondary schools to set up specific in-school programs for learning disabled students using the eight percent monies going to state education agencies. The JTPA presents a great opportunity for learning disabled students to receive job training skills. However, this opportunity will not be recognized unless teachers, parents and others get involved.

Interagency linkages can be initiated by any number of agencies or individuals seeking cooperation and help in providing services to a target group such as learning disabled students. The *Handbook on Developing Effective Linking Strategies,* by Tindall, Gugerty, Getzel, Salin, Wacker, and Crowley (1982), provides a guide in development and implementation of interagency linkages. A specific process for facilitating interagency linkages at the local level in Wisconsin was developed by Tindall and Gugerty (1982).

STEP FOUR:
PROVIDE HELP TO VOCATIONAL AND OTHER EDUCATORS

The State of the Art on how to enroll and help learning disabled students participate in vocational education and job training programs has greatly improved in the past three years. Research dealing specifically with the learning problems of adolescents and adults have made major contributions which can be utilized in inservice and preservice of personnel in vocational education and job training programs. This step will attempt to help vocational and regular educators develop vocational programs which will successfully prepare the learning disabled students for employment. Modifications in teaching strategies and techniques are addressed. Step Five on skill development for the LD is directed at the skills which the LD student must accomplish. Many of the Step Five skills can be integrated into the daily vocational instruction. Therefore this step should integrate information from the other steps.

Vocational teachers and others may not know how to identify learning disabled students or the characteristics of learning disabled students. Informal assessment techniques will help sensitize teachers to these characteristics. Three informal assessment instruments are included here: Table 11.1 What is Your Learning Style, Table 11.2 Tests for Three Types of Learning, and Table 11.3 Learning Disability Assessment Checklist for Teachers.

These checklists can be filled out by teachers or given to students as appropriate. These are informal and not normed and should be used as indicators only. In addition to the information contained in the three checklists, teachers need some of the following information about learning disabilities as discussed by Deshler and others.

1. More than 85 percent of LD adolescents exhibit problems in test taking, study skills, and other areas.
2. LD high school students performed more poorly than a high achieving group of students in note taking, monitoring errors, test taking, scanning a textbook passage and listening comprehension.
3. A large number of students in LD programs have significant deficiencies in general academic ability, reading, writing, mathematics and study skills.

Other characteristics may surface such as the discovery of problems in sequencing materials, eye-hand coordination, problems in visual and auditory perception and verbal and manual expression. LD students commonly have problems in assimilating, organizing and transferring information. Other common problems are the reversal of letters and numbers, spacing in written material, illegible handwriting, completing written assignments and reading levels. LD students may show low self esteem, which may manifest itself in poor attendance, and behavioral problems.

After becoming aware of what to look for in LD identification, vocational teachers need strategies and techniques to incorporate into their instruction which will help compensate for the learning disability. Learning disabled students with little if any reading and writing skills need ways to compensate for their deficiencies. Some methods which will assist in the compensation process are:

1. Allow the tape recording of lectures and materials.
2. Let the LD student use a typewriter for papers or responses to the teacher.
3. Utilize word processors. Teachers can type in rough ideas from the LD student and utilize the word processor to develop appropriate paragraphs and papers.
4. Help the students circumvent problems.
5. Provide study guides and advance organizers.
6. Check to see if the students understand directions.
7. Provide frequent feedback to the students.
8. Utilize questioning and discussion and other teaching techniques more often in lieu of the lecture.
9. Develop alternatives to listening by increasing the use of visual and hands on instruction.
10. Provide alternative tests and test feedback modes.
11. Provide computer assisted instruction.
12. Encourage teacher/student interaction.
13. Help the student take the initiative in recognizing the need for assistance and in seeking out assistance.
14. Help the student develop good study habits.
15. Color code the text for the student.
16. Use an alternate form of instruction, Wiseman and Hartwell (1980).
17. Develop a cooperative note taking system in class.

Teaching Modes

Vocational teachers need to teach in the modes which the LD student learns. The learning mode might be determined through informal assessment techniques or the information might be acquired through the formal evaluations administered by the school psychologist. Listed below are some helps for developing instruction in the visual, auditory, and tactile modes.

Table 11.1
What Is Your Learning Style?

List A

_____ 1. People say you have terrible handwriting.

_____ 2. You don't like silent filmstrips, pantomimes, or charades.

_____ 3. You would rather perform (or listen to) music than do (or view) art, and you would rather listen to a tape than look at a filmstrip.

_____ 4. You sometimes leave out words when writing, or sometimes you get words or letters backwards.

_____ 5. You can spell out loud better than when you have to write it down.

_____ 6. You remember things you talk about in class much better than things you have to read.

_____ 7. You dislike copying material from the blackboard or bulletin boards.

_____ 8. You like jokes or riddles better than cartoons or crossword puzzles.

_____ 9. You like games with lots of action or noise better than checkers or most other board games.

_____ 10. You understand better when you read aloud.

_____ 11. Sometimes you make math mistakes because you don't notice the sign or because you read the numbers or directions wrong.

_____ 12. It seems like you are the last one to notice something new—e.g., that the classroom was painted or that there is a new bulletin board display.

_____ 13. Map activities are just not your thing.

_____ 14. You must struggle to keep neat notes and records.

_____ 15. You use your fingers as a pointer when you read.

_____ 16. You frequently hum or whistle to yourself when you are working.

_____ 17. Sometimes your eyes just "bother" you, but your eye tests come out all right, or you have glasses which your eye doctor says are just right for you.

_____ 18. You hate to read from ditto sheets, especially blotty ones.

_____ 19. "Matching test" questions are a problem to sort out (over and above not knowing some of the answers.)

_____ 20. Sometimes when you read you mix up words that look similar (pill-pull, bale-hale).

_____ Score: Number Answered YES

List B

_____ 1. It seems like you always have to ask somebody to repeat what he or she just said.

_____ 2. Sometimes you may find yourself "tuned out"—staring out the window maybe when you were really trying to pay attention to something.

Table 11.1 (*cont.*)

_____ 3. Often you know what you want to say, but you just can't think of the words. Sometimes you may even be accused of "talking with your hands," or calling something a "thingamajig" or a "whatyacallit."

_____ 4. You have been in speech therapy at some time previously.

_____ 5. You may have trouble understanding a person who is talking to you when you are unable to watch the persons face while he or she is speaking.

_____ 6. You would rather receive directions in a demonstration format than in spoken form.

_____ 7. When you watch TV or listen to the radio, someone is always asking you to turn it down.

_____ 8. Your family says that you say, "huh?", too much.

_____ 9. You would rather demonstrate how to do something than make a speech.

_____ 10. Spoken words that sound similar (bell, bill, pin or pen) give you trouble. Sometimes you can't tell them apart.

_____ 11. You have trouble remembering things unless you write them down.

_____ 12. You like board games such as checkers better than listening games.

_____ 13. Sometimes you make mistakes in speaking (like saying "he got expended from school").

_____ 14. You like art work better than music.

_____ 15. You have to go over most of the alphabet to remember whether, e, g, m, comes before r.

_____ 16. You like it better when someone *shows* you what to do, rather than just telling you.

_____ 17. You can do a lot of things that are hard to explain with words — like fixing machines or doing macrame.

_____ 18. You usually answer questions with "yes" or "no" rather than with complete sentences.

_____ 19. Often you forget to give verbally received messages (such as telephone messages) to people unless you write them.

_____ 20. You are always drawing little pictures on the edges of your papers, or doodling on scratch paper.

_____ Score: Number Answered YES

If list A is very much higher than list B, the person in question could be considered an auditory learner. If list B is much higher, it indicates that the person in question might be considered a visual learner. If both lists are high, this person's best learning mode would probably be touching and doing.

The above material is drawn from Hayes, Marnell L. *The Tune-in, Turned-on Book About Learning Problems.* San Rafael, Cal.: Academic Therapy Publications, 1974.

Table 11.2
Tests for Three Types of Learning

Test Ground Rules

To give the test, you need:

1. A group of not more than 15 students as it is difficult to observe more than that at one time.

2. A list of the students' names which you can mark as you observe their reactions.
   V = Visual Learner
   A = Audio Learner
   K = Kinesthetic Learner

Reactions to watch for:

Visual Learners will usually close their eyes or look at the ceiling as they try to recall a visual picture.

Audio Learners will move their lips or whisper as they try to memorize.

Kinesthetic Learners will use their fingers to count off items or write in the air.

Conducting the Test

Start by telling your students that you are going to give them a test to determine what kind of learners they are: *Visual, Audio, or Kinesthetic.*

This test consists of pretending that the students are going to the toolroom to get some tools for you. (The list should either include items appropriate to your class, or should be general, such as items to pick up at a grocery store.) First, you will write the list on the board, allowing the students to watch you, but they must not copy it. Next, you will give them the list orally. You will not write it and neither must they. Then, you will dictate the list to them orally and they will write it down.

After each presentation, you will ask your students to repeat the list to you if they wish. If a student is not able to repeat the list, tell him or her not to worry. The response to your request should be voluntary and the list does not have to be given back in order.

The specific test or tests in which the student has the highest recall is a reinforcement of his native way of learning. However, the symptoms are the prime indication.

First Presentation	List I
1. Write the list on the board while the students are watching. Do not let them write.	Hammer
2. Allow students to view the list for approximately one minute while observing their reactions. Mark the symptoms after the students' names.	Pliers
Symptoms: Visual Learners — Close their eyes or look at the ceiling. (V after name)	Crescent Wrench
Audio Learners — Move their lips or whisper. (A after name)	
Kinesthetic Learners — Count the items on their fingers or write in the air. (K after name)	Paint Brush

Table 11.2 (*cont.*)

3. Erase the list.	Screwdriver
4. Ask, "Who would like to repeat the items to me?"	Welding Rods
5. Observe that the Visual Learners will volunteer first.	Level
6. Call on them to recite <u>orally,</u> one at a time, (Note that after a few students have recited, a few more timid hands will go up. These usually are *Audio Learners* who have learned the list, not from seeing it, but from hearing the other students say the items.	Battery Tester
7. As you notice a student's symptoms, make "V," "A," or "K" after the student's name.	

Second Presentation	List II
1. Dictate the list <u>orally,</u> (no writing by either teacher or students). Repeat the dictation a second time, pausing for a moment after each item.	Tape Measure Square
2. <u>Observe</u> that the *Visual Learners* will close their eyes to try to SEE the items. The *Audio Learners* will whisper each item as you dictate it. The *Kinesthetic Learners* will use their hands to mark off the number of items or will write in the air.	Screwdriver Chalk Line
3. Ask, "Who would like to repeat the list?"	Vise Grip
4. The audio learners will be the most eager to respond, although other students will try to repeat the items you have dictated.	Level Hammer
5. Make appropriate notation of "V," "A," or "K" after the students' names as you notice their reactions.	Pliers

Third Presentation	List III
1. Tell the students to have pencil and paper ready to <u>write</u> the list as you dictate it <u>orally.</u> Tell them you will not count spelling. In fact, spell the words as you dictate.	Chalk Line Plumb Bob
2. After you have finished dictating the list, tell the students to rewrite the list, and to look at the one they have written from your dictation.	Hand Saw
3. When they have finished rewriting the list, tell them to turn the paper over and <u>write the list from memory.</u>	Tape Measure
4. After they have finished, check to see which students have been able to repeat the list wholly or in part.	Welding Rods Power Drill
5. Notice that students who are unsuccessful in either the first or second presentation of the test are frequently the first ones finished.	Pliers Square

(The test may be repeated using numbers. Most students have a different form of recall for numbers than they have for words.)

Adapted from Baxter, Wynn, *Magnetic Patterns of the English Language.* Arlington, Va.: Virtitas Publications, 1975.

Table 11.3
Learning Disability Assessment Checklist for Teachers

Note the frequency with which students exhibit the following behaviors. Consistent behaviors such as these may indicate the presence of a learning disability.

Reading

1. Reading is mechanical, without expression
2. Guesses words based upon a few letters (the first, last letters)
3. Reads unevenly
4. Reads past mistakes without attempting to correct errors regardless of meaning
5. Reads very slowly, sounding out words while reading
6. Repeats words, loses place, goes back to find place
7. Unable to blend sounds together to get words
8. Moves lips during silent reading (subvocalizes)
9. Does not seem to understand what he or she has read, despite ability to read fluently
10. Comprehends what is read to him or her better than what he or she reads by self
11. Does not read willingly

Writing

1. Does not organize ideas into meaningful paragraphs
2. Punctuates incorrectly
3. Does not write complete sentences
4. Reverses letters in a sentence; e.g., calm-clam; girl-gril; dirt-drit; saw-was
5. Spells phonetically and writes nonphonetic words incorrectly; e.g., thier, howse, eaite, etc.
6. Erases, crosses out, messes up work with scribbling when making corrections in written work
7. Does not write within lines on paper or indent paragraphs; follows incorrect form for writing
8. Written work deteriorates when under pressure of time testing or when work is long or demanding
9. Work shows poor placement on a page. Work (especially math or drawings) is spaced erratically on the paper
10. Avoids written work though highly verbal in class
11. Oral performance far exceeds written work

Speaking

1. Does not articulate clearly and understandably
2. Does not pronounce ending sounds in words correctly
3. Has tendency to confuse words he or she hears: "profane" becomes "propane," "animal" becomes "aminal," "very" becomes "revy"
4. Speaks quickly and nervously; thus is hard to follow or understand at times
5. Answers questions tangentially and has difficulty in getting to the point
6. Has difficulty finding the correct words when speaking
7. Interrupts self when speaking; distracts self and changes the subject; is fragmented and disorganized

Listening

1. Does not seem to listen to instructions
2. Does not attend to what is happening in class
3. Seems to misunderstand language

Math

1. Does not understand place value of numbers
2. Has difficulty in spatial concepts and measurement
3. Does not understand borrowing and carrying in math
4. Cannot remember math facts (addition and multiplication) and recall them automatically
5. Has difficulty with math problems that are written out in sentence form

Attitude

1. Does the student follow through on assigned work, or become disorganized and fail to complete assignments?
2. Does the learner often appear lethargic or apathetic, yawn, appear bored and without energy?
3. Does the student seem to feel inadequate or negative, and put self down?

Table 11.3 (cont.)

4. Does he or she tend to be a loner? 5. Does the student handle frustration by acting out aggressively? 6. Does the learner shy away from anything new academically, socially, athletically, for fear of failure?	7. Does the student have a shorter attention span than most of his or her peers? 8. Does the student claim not to need help? Avoid coming for help after school or during tutorials, for fear of appearing "stupid" or a "dummy"?

Adapted from Weiss, Helen Ginandes, and Martin S. Weiss, *A Survival Manual: Case Studies and Suggestions for the Learning Disabled Teenager* (Great Barrington, Mass.: Treehouse Associates, 1976), pp. 68–71.

Teach in the Visual Mode

1. Develop mind pictures and vivid images.
2. Make notes to self.
3. Underline or highlight in color.
4. Use charts or graphs.
5. Provide actual materials.
6. Use pointers, guides.
7. Decongest materials.

Teach in the Auditory Mode

1. Use audio cassettes.
2. Listen to recorded texts.
3. Say it, repeat it.
4. Try to hear it.
5. Eliminate visual interference.
6. Avoid complex situations.

Teach in the Tactile Mode

1. Provide hands on materials.
2. Use body muscles, squeeze ball, toe tap.
3. Study position changes, sit, stand, walk.
4. Use metronome.

Many researchers have addressed the issue of learning style and learning modes. McCarthy (1980) studies learning styles and summarized the learning style characteristics as (1) Innovative Learners; (2) Analytic Learners; (3) Common Sense Learners; and (4) Dynamic Learners. She considered all four styles equally valuable with strengths and weaknesses in each style. The most important learning style is the one in which the student feels most comfortable. McCarthy also conducted research on the functions of the left hemisphere and right hemisphere of the brain. The left brain does verbal things and the right brain does visual-spatial things. Vocational education and job training personnel need to realize the consequences of being a left brain or right brain learner and develop the appropriate strategies for helping a left brain or right brain learner. The goal of the instruction should be to help students develop the whole brain. Instruction which will assist students who are analytic and who are intuitive needs to be developed.

Listening, Thinking, Speaking, Writing, Reading, and Math

Although vocational teachers may not think about teaching listening, thinking, speaking, writing, reading and math skills they can make the LD student aware of the necessity of these skills and integrate them into the daily instruction. Helps for improving these skills are summarized below:

Thinking Helps
Tell about a task
Observe and tell
Put together — take apart
Troubleshoot
Plan major events
Plan field trips
Solve a problem

Speaking Helps
Enroll student in speech class
Demonstrate and explain
Think before speaking
Make tapes and listen
Provide separate study area

Listening Helps
Gestures
Voices
Double words
Pauses
Sequences
Major Points
Glossaries
Encourage Questions

Writing Helps
Write ideas
Draw pictures
Express ideas orally
Get classmates notes
Give oral exams
Develop note taking skill

Reading Helps
Get a diagnosis
Use existing ability
Teach note taking
Audio tapes
Demonstrations
Glossary
Explain
Provide other ways

Math Helps
Learn measurement units
Calculators
Visuals
Tactile materials
Coordinate math and
     vocational education

Using Muscles to Help Learning

Barsch (1982) has worked with LD students in the use of muscles to increase learning. Changing body postures when studying every 15 minutes helps. Memorizing while walking may be difficult but the material is remembered. Squeezing a rubber ball while studying has also proven successful for some students.

Teaching the LD Students that Skills are Transferrable

Skills which are learned in a secondary or postsecondary vocational setting can be transferred to other vocational situations and on to employment environments. The idea that skills needed in the classroom and shop are similar to those needed in the work place may not be readily apparent to the learning disabled student. Therefore, emphasis on the transfer of those skills which accompany the actual vocational skill needs to be made. As an example, a vocational graduate specializing in the repair and maintenance of bicycles could utilize the following skills in a job at a bicycle repair shop.

1. Questioning
2. Listening
3. Writing
4. Generalizing
5. Monitor errors
6. Understand charts, graphs, tasks
7. Read a manual

Computer Assisted Instruction for Learning Disabled Students

Microcomputer assisted instruction for learning disabled students is at a primative stage of development. Relatively few special and vocational educators have incorporated CAI into their curricula for LD students. The CAI which is in use does not necessarily incorporate educational psychology into the format and does not utilize the rapidly advancing capabilities of the equipment.

Computer programmers may not understand educational processes well enough to develop effective software. On the other hand, the majority of learning disability personnel may not be computer literate or capable of programming computers effectively. The lack of training and coordination is compounded by the lack of effective software.

Most CAI authorities recommend purchasing quality computers with sufficient capacity to cover the bulk of the software which is available. The cost of the hardware will be offset by an expanded curriculum, improved academic performance, a more efficient utilization of resources, increased motivation, decrease in LD students failures and a saving of time.

Unfortunately the most popular usages of CAI in the classroom now consists of drill and practice, and tutorial formats. Formats which stress problem solving, simulation, provide challenge, curiosity, imagination, high student interaction, and are graphically illustrated are seldom available. The utilization of computers and video disks is an untapped resource at this time.

CAI has some very positive attributes which make it attractive for use with LD students. It can: be a supplement to instruction, improve achievement, be an informal reacter, reduce instructional time, can set a pace, can be superior to a text, provide quick feedback, can tutor, provide surprise and imagination, quiz and test and will not embarrass the student. Effective CAI programs will: build in student control, individualize, modulize, help master difficult tasks, be multisensory in approach, be at a student level, have supportive materials, use interaction, use dialog devices, provide key word acceptance and give student feedback.

CAI must focus on conceptual teaching and be a part of the curriculum. It is not a panacea and it will not replace the teacher and the human interaction necessary in teaching LD students. Teachers will need to use a year or more in preparation for CAI instruction. This time should be spent on becoming computer literate, in selecting CAI software and in incorporating CAI into the existing curricula. It does not appear practical at this point for the LD teaching personnel to develop their own CAI programs due to the great amount of time needed for this activity. Time can best be spent in selecting from the available software and in making the needs of LD students known to the computer programmers. CAI is a rapidly advancing technology and LD students will benefit if their teachers will prepare now to incorporate CAI into the regular curricula.

STEP FIVE:
SKILL DEVELOPMENT FOR LEARNING DISABLED STUDENTS

Part Four addressed the strategies which vocational teachers and others can use in teaching the LD student. Step Five addresses some skills which the LD student must acquire. The best possible job of teaching may not be successful unless the LD student possesses learning and coping skills.

The independence of the LD student must be fostered. They must become more effective learners and function as independent learners to the maximum extent possible. An ability to solve problems, transfer learning, meet recurring demands which require similar response and a general reduction in the level of handicap will greatly increase the LD person's effectiveness as a student or an employee.

Functional Survival Skills

Basic to the education of the learning disabled student are "Survival Skills." These skills are especially important as the LD student seeks employment. Some of these survival skills are (1) how to get on the right bus; (2) How to read want ads; (3) How to fill out tax forms; (4) How to listen to suggestions and criticisms from teachers and employers; (5) How to use a telephone; (6) How to interview for a job; and (7) How to get along with peers and coworkers.

Teaching the LD Student How to Learn

Recent studies at the Institute for Research in Learning Disabilities (IRLD) at the University of Kansas have explored learning strategy interventions for adolescents (Deshler *et al.* 1982). Although IRLD researchers did not stress vocational education, the studies have implications for vocational teachers and vocational curricula. How LD students learn is important to all subject areas. IRLD researchers suggested that if the LD students basic skills level was fourth grade or above, a learning strategy approach could be used. If the LD student was below fourth grade level the approach should be intense compensation skills and intense skill remediation. They further suggested that the less severe LD student may get along with one resource room class per day. However, the more severe LD student needs an intense input over a period of time. IRLD researchers have been able to teach nearly 100 percent of the 70 LD students in their research group a learning strategy.

Nine learning strategies were included in the study. Vocational teachers could teach some of these strategies with a little additional preparation time. The results would be well worth the effort and the non-LD students would also benefit. The other strategies could be taught by the LD advocate or special education teacher. The school's LD support service could work with the vocational teacher in the classroom to help the LD student learn these strategies. The learning strategies are provided below:

1. Word Definition
2. Paraphrasing
3. Self Questioning
4. Multipass—attacking textbook chapters
   (Survey, Size Up, Sort Out)
5. Sentence Writing
6. Paragraph Organization
7. Error Monitoring
8. Listening
9. Note Taking

The IRLD staff at the University of Kansas also developed a method to help teach the strategies. Points One to Nine below outline their method:

1. Determine Current Learning Habits
2. Describe New Learning Strategy
3. Model the Strategy
4. Verbally Rehearse Strategy
5. Practice Strategy (Controlled Reading Level)
6. Give Feedback
7. Practice Strategy (Vocational Materials)
8. Give Feedback
9. Test

Error Correction

Specific details of the strategy for error correction are provided at this point. The error correction strategy works and is a valuable tool for learning disabled vocational students to acquire. There are four tasks to be done to initiate the error correction strategy (Schumaker 1981):

1. Read each sentence separately
2. Ask COPS questions
3. Circle errors, correct error
4. Ask for help

The COPS questions are then asked and the resulting activities carried out. The four COPS questions follow:

C Capitalize first word, proper names
O Overall appearance (spacing, legibility, indentation, neatness, complete sentences)
P Punctuation (commas, periods, ?)
S Spelling (are all words correctly spelled?)

Six additional steps were devised by the IRLD staff to round out the error monitoring strategy. They are:

1. Use every other line (rough draft)
2. Ask COPS questions
3. Circle errors, add correction
4. Ask for help
5. Make final draft
6. Reread final

This error correction strategy has proven successful and could be readily incorporated into the vocational curriculum. This and other learning strategies would be an asset to the LD student. These strategies would promote independence and would be transferrable to other subjects and life situations.

STEP SIX: PROVIDE PLACEMENT SERVICES

The ultimate goal of vocational education and job training for the LD student at both the secondary and postsecondary levels is the achievement of employment and the involvement in a meaningful career. Assuming that we are successful in the vocational education and training of the LD student the next step is employment. Hopefully the LD student would be familiar with many jobs and career areas so that he or she could make the appropriate employment decisions. He or she should have participated in a variety of pre-employment activities such as job exploration, work study, on the job training, apprenticeship training, or job shadowing. Education to work activities such as role playing in interviewing, filling out job applications, job seeking skills, peer and employer relationships and how to keep a job should have been experienced.

There are volumes of materials written on job placement strategies and techniques. However, it is sometimes best to consider the experience of persons who have been successful over a period of many years in placing LD students. Thanos (1982) provided a list of twelve activities and policies which he used successfully for several years in the job placement of LD students.

1. Know the student well. You will be working closely with employers and must know the product which you are selling, both for the employer's benefit and for the LD student's benefit.
2. Help the LD student explore jobs. This may involve the joint reading

of want ads, help in writing letters, and acquiring job specific information.
3. Visit the work area. See first hand what tasks are involved and get a feeling for the work climate. Note any positive or negative factors.
4. Talk with employers and employees. Get a view from both sides of the job. Make evaluations of the job and whether or not your client would be welcome, could succeed or advance.
5. Do not stereotype the LD student. No two LD students are alike. Convey this to the employer and be specific about each LD student.
6. Be available to the employer. Let the employer know that you can help resolve conflicts and can provide advice on how the LD student will function effectively on the job.
7. Be honest with employers. Provide the employer with an accurate representation of the LD person's strengths, competencies and weaknesses if appropriate. Misrepresentations will close doors in a hurry.
8. Provide steady, persistant, honest, cooperative hard work over time. Good placement counselors really like their jobs, the employers they work with and the students they place.
9. Remember that a high turnover rate of job placement counselors may be detrimental to the cause. LD persons are especially vulnerable to counselor turnover.
10. Help the LD person to enjoy and anticipate success. Set short term goal to anticipate such as first paycheck, first raise, first month, first job evaluation.
11. Help the LD person to establish a meaningful career. Placement is more than just helping the LD person get a job. LD persons need advice on how to advance, when to change jobs, etc.
12. Provide assistance over a long period of time. Make yourself available to the person for the same length of time you hold your own job or on your next job if you are in the same geographical area.

STEP SEVEN: PLAN FOR LIFETIME EDUCATION

The job situation in the United States is under constant change. Jobs become obsolete and economic conditions create layoffs. The new technology and high technology occupations may require additional education and training. Education and updated or new training will be required for job advancement and reemployment. Failure to acquire more education may result in unemployment, underemployment, and lower wages.

Learning disabled persons must acquire the philosophy that continuous education is a way of life. The average age of persons in postsecondary vocational schools and other job training institutions is rising. To help the LD person cope with this situation, they will need skills on how to identify appropriate next steps. Skills in how to seek out, enroll in or explore new jobs and new educational opportunities will be important. Knowledge that postsecondary schools, employment offices and other services are available to all persons will provide a starting place when jobs fail and economic conditions create unemployment situations. It is therefore necessary that any stigma about continued education be removed.

SUMMARY

Education and training for learning disabled students will require much hard work and planning on the part of both special and vocational educators and other members of the school and business community. We need to start with the assessment and evaluation of the LD student and then develop the appropriate support services and interagency linkages to assist in the delivery of the vocational education and training.

The state of the art on how to teach LD students has made a rapid advancement during the last five years. The strategies and techniques on how to teach adolescents and adults is becoming more clear. Vocational and job training teachers need to become aware of these strategies and incorporate them into the curricula. It is apparent that the best job of teaching will not create successful learners. LD students must obtain skills to help them become effective and independent learners.

After the appropriate employment skills have been acquired, LDs need specific help in locating employment and maintaining employment which leads to meaningful careers. Finally LDs need to realize that education is a lifetime task and that there will be a need for future and ongoing education.

REFERENCES

Barsch, J. *Learning with Your Muscles*. Ventura, Cal.: Ventura College, 1982.

Bender, L. *Bender-Gestalt. Visual Motor Gestalt Test*. New York: Grune and Stratton, c/o Academic Press, 1953.

Brown, L. S. "Vocational Assessment for Learning Disabled Students." T. H. Hohenshil and W. T. Anderson eds., *Secondary School Psychological Services: Focus on Vocational Assessment Procedures for Handicapped Students*. Blacksburg, Va.: Conference proceedings, 1982.

Career Ability Placement Survey, San Diego, Cal.: Edits Publishers, 1976.

Clark, F. L. *Major Research Findings of the University of Kansas Institute for Research in Learning Disabilities.* Lawrence, Kans.: University of Kansas, Institute for Research in Learning Disabilities, 1981.

Congressional Record. House, Conference Report on 52036, p. 13. September 28, 1982.

Cook, L. D. "The Adolescent with a Learning Disability: A Developmental Perspective." *Adolescence* 14 (1979): 697–707.

Department of Labor. *Interest Inventory.* Washington, D.C.: U.S. Government Printing Office, 1979.

Deshler, D., J. B. Schumaker, G. R. Alley, M. M. Warner, and F. L. Clark. "Learning Disabilities in Adolescent and Young Adult Populations: Research Implications." *Focus on Exceptional Children* 5, 1 (Sept. 1982).

Dunn, L. M., and F. C. Markwardt. "Peabody Individual Achievement Test." New York: Psychological Corporation, 1970.

Educational Industrial Testing Service. *California Occupational Preference System.* San Diego, Cal.: 1974.

Grisafe, J. P. *Vocational Assessment Handbook.* Riverside, Cal.: Office of Riverside County Superintendent of Schools, January 1983.

Hooper, P. G. "Guidance and Counseling, Potential Impact on Youth Employment. *Journal of Career Education* (1980): 270–287.

Kapes, J. T., and M. M. Mastie. *"A Counselor's Guide to Vocational Guidance Instruments."* Alexandria, Va.: National Vocational Guidance Association, 1982.

Keystone Telebinocular. Davenport, Iowa: Keystone View Co., 1945.

Kirk, S. A., J. J. McCarthy, and W. D. Kirk. *Illinois Test of Psycholinguistic Abilities, Revised.* Los Angeles, Calif.: Western Psychological Services.

McCarthy, B. *The 4MAT System, Teaching Learning Styles with Right/Left Mode Techniques.* Oak Brook, Ill.: Excel, 1980.

McCray, P. M. *Vocational Evaluation and Assessment in School Settings.* Menomonie, Wisc.: University of Wisconsin-Stout, Vocational Rehabilitation Institute, Research and Training Center, 1982.

Ohio Vocational Interest Survey. New York: Psychological Corporation, 1970.

Program for Assessing Youth Employability Skills. Princeton, N.J.: Educational Testing Service, 1979.

Roach, E. G., and N. C. Kephart. *Purdue Perceptual Motor Survey.* Columbus, Ohio: Charles E. Merrill, 1966.

Schumaker, J. B., D. D. Deshler, P. Denton, G. R. Alley, F. L. Clark, and M. M. Warner. *Multipass: A Learning Strategy for Improving Reading Comprehension.* Lawrence, Kan.: University of Kansas Institute for Research in Learning Disabilities, 1981.

Schumaker, J. B., D. D. Deshler, S. Nolan, F. L. Clark, G. R. Alley, and M. M. Warner. *Error Monitoring: A Learning Strategy for Improving Academic Performance of LD Adolescents.* Lawrence, Kan.: University of Kansas Institute for Research in Learning Disabilities, 1981.

Singer/Career Systems. 1333 Lawrence Expressway, Bldg. 100, Suite 109, Santa Clara, Cal. 95051.

Slingerland, B. H. *Slingerland Screening Tests for Identifying Children with Specific Language Disability.* Los Angeles, Cal.: Western Psychological Services, 1970.

Strong-Campbell Interest Inventory. Stanford, Cal.: Stanford University Press, 1977.

Talent Assessment Program. Jacksonville, Fla.: Talent Assessment, Inc., 1980.

Texas Education Agency, Department of Occupational Education and Technology Research Coordinating Unit. *Vocational Assessment of Students with Special Needs. An Implementation Manual.* Austin, Tex., 1982.

Thanos, G. Personal communication, Ventura College, Ventura, Cal., 1982.

Tindall, L. W., and J. Gugerty. *Improving Vocational Education and Employment for Handicapped People: A Process for Facilitating Interagency Linkages in Wisconsin.* Madison, Wisc.: University of Wisconsin-Madison, Vocational Studies Center, 1982.

Tindall, L. W., J. Gugerty, E. E. Getzel, J. Salin, G. B. Wacker, and C. B. Crowley. *Vocational Education Models for Linking Agencies Serving the Handicapped: Handbook on Developing Effective Linking Strategies.* Madison, Wisc.: University of Wisconsin—Madison, Vocational Studies Center, 1982.

Trevitt, M. Personal communication. Santa Ana, Cal.: Santa Ana College, 1982.

Vacc, N. A., and J. I. Bardon. *Assessment and Appraisal: Issues, Practices and Programs, A Special Journal Issue of Measurement and Evaluation in Guidance.* Alexandria, Va.: American Association for Counseling and Development, 1982.

Valpar Component Work Samples. Tucson, Ariz., 1978.

Vocational Research Institute, Philadelphia, Penn.: Jewish Employment and Vocational Service, 1973.

Warner, M. M., and G. R. Alley. *Teaching Learning Disabled Junior High Students to use Visual Imagery as a Strategy for Facilitating Recall of Reading Passages.* Lawrence, Kan.: University of Kansas Institute for Research in Learning Disabilities, 1981.

Wechsler, D. *Wechsler Adult Intelligence Scale, Revised.* New York: Psychological Corporation, 1955.

Wechsler, D. *Wechsler Intelligence Scale for Children, Revised.* New York: Psychological Corporation, 1974.

White, W. J., J. T. Schumaker, M. M. Warner, G. R. Alley, and D. D. Deshler. *The Current Status of Young Adults Identified as Learning Disabled During Their School Career.* Lawrence, Kan.: University of Kansas, Institute for Research in Learning Disabilities, 1981.

Wide Range Interest Opinion Test. Wilmington, Del.: Jastak Assessment Systems, Inc., 1970.

Wiseman, D. E., and L. K. Hartwell. *Parallel Alternate Curriculum, A Planning Model for Secondary Level Instructors.* Tempe, Ariz.: Arizona State University, Department of Special Education, 1980.

Woodcock, R. W., and M. B. Johnson. *Woodcock-Johnson Psycho-Educational Battery.* Hingham, Mass.: Teaching Resources Corp., 1977.

12

A Neuropsychological Model
for Vocational Planning
for Learning Disabled Students

Cathy F. Telzrow and Lawrence C. Hartlage

Unlike many disease entities which are based on specific laboratory and clinical findings, a learning disability is defined in the federal regulations as a presence of a severe discrepancy between intellectual ability and academic achievement in one of seven areas. In several states the determination of a severe discrepancy is based in part on the application of various statistical formulae (Elliott 1981; Reynolds 1981; Shepard 1980). Although the diagnosis of learning disabilities for the purpose of educational identification and placement requires the demonstration of a specified discrepancy between measured ability (IQ) and achievement (in basic reading skills or mathematics calculation), there is increasing evidence that the observed discrepancy can be attributed to some type of neurologically based limitation in information processing, perhaps of a structural (Geschwind 1979) or neurochemical nature. The field of learning disabilities, therefore, represents an amalgam of the neurologic and psychologic sciences, since the presumed etiology is of neurologic origin, and the eligibility requirements rely upon psychological assessment. As a result of this partnership between neurology and psychology in the field of learning disabilities, neuropsychology would appear to represent the most viable diagnostic procedure. This article will illustrate how data derived from neuropsychological assessment can be utilized to develop long range educational programs with an eye toward meaningful vocational planning and, ultimately, optimal functional independence.

SOURCES OF NEUROPSYCHOLOGICAL DATA

General Level of Intellectual Functioning

While there has been a tendency in some educational circles to eschew measured intelligence levels as irrelevant or at best minimally important for

143

educational and vocational planning, the level of intellectual functioning continues to represent the best single predictor of academic performance (Hartlage 1979). The individual IQ test is significantly more sensitive to subtle differences in central nervous system integrity than comparatively imprecise medical measures (Hartlage and Hartlage 1977), including recent advances such as the PET scan and BEAM. As a result, learning disabled children who demonstrate no hard clinical findings on neurologic examination may show specific deficits in cognitive functioning when psychological test scores are analyzed (Lechtenberg 1982).

Although the federal definition of specific learning disabilities lists mental retardation as one of several exclusionary criteria, and LD children generally are described as those who have average or above intelligence, in practice the IQ test scores for children identified learning disabled might range as low as 70 and as high as 140 or above. The absolute level of mental ability of individuals with learning disabilities is an extremely important consideration in the development of realistic educational and vocational plans. The underlying premise of the ability-achievement discrepancy model inherent in the federal definition relies upon the predictive relationship between the two types of measured performance. It is possible, this model asserts, to predict levels of achievement on the basis of intellectual functioning. The implication of this relationship between ability and achievement for educational planning is that academic expectancies can be derived and used to guide educational objectives. The student who has an average IQ score, for example, might require quite different educational objectives from one who has an IQ of 85, or of 140. In addition, the theoretical growth curve of the ability-achievement interaction suggests that the difference between the child with a low average to borderline IQ score and his or her average-IQ peer widens with time (Meisels and Anastasiow 1980). Thus, while the beginning first grader with an IQ of 90 might be expected to achieve within average grade level expectancies, by third grade the predicted attainment level for this student is a year below grade placement (Hartlage 1979). Through middle school, junior high, and high school years, the range of expected achievement levels for children of varying abilities continues to widen, such that a tenth grade teacher with a group of children with IQ scores between 85 and 140 might reasonably have children with expected achievement levels between sixth grade and average adult.

Children with learning disabilities complicate the ability-achievement expectancy curve, since by definition they do not achieve at expected levels. Nevertheless, intellectual performance levels represent a probable, though not absolute, indicator of achievement potential. The general level of intellectual functioning also represents an important prognostic variable, in helping predict the degree to which learning disabled children are capable of adjusting to and compensating for their handicaps. The most favorable outcomes for educational and vocational adjustment in populations of learning disabled children are associated with the highest-ability group of students (Buda 1981), who demonstrate superior ability to acquire adaptive responses.

General intellectual functioning level represents one of the earliest and most psychometrically precise sources of data available to parents in their efforts toward vocational planning for their learning disabled children. Such information can be used to assist parents in their analysis of the wide range of vocational opportunities, and can be used to generate an initial pool of vocationally feasible goals. An individual with an IQ of 140, for example, with a significant learning disability involving counting and mathematical skills (dyscalculia), may still have performance levels within the average range, since, with an IQ of 140, computational skills at a level appropriate to an IQ of 100 represents a significant discrepancy. Conversely, an individual with an IQ of 100 and computational skill appropriate to an IQ of 60 has the same absolute magnitude of discrepancy between ability and achievement, but would be limited to jobs not requiring computational skills much above the third grade level.

Information Processing Deficits

While overall intellectual functioning is an important reflection of general neuropsychological integrity, a single measure of cognitive performance may mask high and low performance points characteristic of many learning disabled children. An alternative source of neuropsychological data utilizes an informationing processing approach to attempt to identify functional strengths and weaknesses in cognitive performance.

Because of the discrete information processing strategies which have been associated with the left and right hemispheres (Bogen 1977), the selection of psychometric instruments which are sensitive to the relative integrity of the two hemispheres is possible (Hartlage 1981). The left hemisphere is uniquely associated with processing linguistic information, and as a result measures of language development are typically utilized to assess left hemisphere functioning (Hartlage and Hartlage 1977, 1982). Due to the specific involvement of the right hemisphere in visuo-spatial processing (Nebes 1974, 1977), psychometric instruments which incorporate tasks of this nature (e.g., constructional praxis tasks) have been associated with right hemisphere functioning (Hartlage and Hartlage 1977).

Other more direct neuropsychological tests which are sensitive to the functioning of the two hemispheres often are employed to enlarge and verify data obtained on psychometric instruments. Tasks of this nature, which may involve a comparison of sensory and motor functioning on the two sides of the body (Hartlage and Hartlage 1982; Reitan and Davison 1974), provide comparatively "pure" data, in that such tasks are culturally non-biased and are not dependent on experience (Hartlage 1981). Examples of such tasks include finger tapping, fingertip number writing, dichotic listening, and visual field tests, all of which compare the relative efficiency of the two sides of the body.

While in most persons, information flows freely from one hemisphere to the other, such that hemispheric specialization contributes to problem solving by a "division of labor" strategy (Levy 1974, 1980), recent research has indicated that the majority of human beings may have a preferred cerebral processing strategy. One of the best lines of supporting evidence for this conclusion comes from specific neuroanatomical studies which have reported asymmetry between the two hemispheres, with one hemisphere being significantly larger. Just as asymmetry of the two sides of the body is apparent upon rather gross external examination (Levy and Levy 1979), these studies have demonstrated that such asymmetry is evident within the human brain as well. Convergent validation has occurred from numerous sources, all demonstrating approximately equal percentages of asymmetry (Galaburda, LeMay, Kemper, and Geschwind 1979; Geschwind and Levitsky 1968). Since these findings have been replicated in populations of stillborn neonates (Witelson and Pallie 1973) and even at the thirty-fourth week of fetal life (Chi, Dooling, and Gilles 1977), it appears quite likely that the observed asymmetry is biologically determined, rather than a result of specific environmental modification.

There is increasing speculation among learning disabilities experts that functional cerebral asymmetry may be of etiologic significance in learning disabilities (Geshwind 1979; Hartlage 1981). Subtypes of specific learning disabilities have been associated with recognized patterns of information processing deficits. Bannatyne (1978), for example, has identified the spatially competent LD child, who is reported to demonstrate adequate visuo spatial (i.e., right hemisphere) skills, while exhibiting deficits in auditory-phonetic, left hemisphere mediated abilities. Similarly, Boder (Boder and Jarrico 1982) has described disabled readers who exhibit auditory-phonetic weaknesses (dysphonetic dyslexics), visuo spatial deficits (dyseidetic dyslexics), and a mixed group demonstrating characteristics of both. A recent study of the neuropsychological features of these dyslexic categories has found increased incidence of specific neuropsychological impairment in the mixed dyslexic group (Telzrow, Century, Redmond, Whittaker, and Zimmerman, in press).

Numerous implications of hemispheric asymmetry of function are apparent, many of which relate to specific educational (Boder 1971; Hartlage 1981; Marcel, Katz, and Smith 1974) and vocational (Hartlage 1981) interventions. In general, the more advanced the level of education, the greater the dependence on the left cerebral hemisphere, since as a child progresses from memorizing shapes and letters to reading for analysis and comprehension, there is increasingly greater emphasis on abilities mediated by the left hemisphere. Thus an individual with poor function of the right hemisphere may have more difficulty in early school grades, and progressively become less academically handicapped as the educational requirements increasingly allow greater use of the comparatively more efficient left hemisphere. Such an individual, however, could be expected to have vocationally limiting deficits if the career goal relied extensively on the visuo spatial sorts of abilities dependent on efficient right hemisphere function. Conversely, an individual with impaired left cerebral hemisphere functioning may not demonstrate apparent learning disabilities in early school grades, but may become relatively more learning disabled with increasing demands on language proficiency. From a vocational aspect, individuals with left hemisphere related learning disabilities such as difficulty with reading, verbal comprehension or expression are obviously limited for work where such skills represent an essential component of job performance.

In addition to specific cognitive deficits observed in learning disabled children, there is increasing evidence that functional cerebral asymmetry is associated with specific behavioral characteristics as well (Hartlage, Telzrow, DeFilippis, Shaw, and Noonan 1983). Since many of these behavioral characteristics are of relevance for worker trait demands, this is an important concept for vocational planning.

Individuals with dysfunctional right hemispheres, in addition to being at risk for visuo spatial learning disabilities and work related problems, tend to be more inclined to use impulsive, less reflective approaches to problem solving, in what neurologists often refer to as "la belle indifference" life styles. An individual with right cerebral hemisphere dysfunction resultant from stroke, for example, may commonly deny any impairment or problem, even though the sequelae have resulted in considerable weakness of the left side of the body or even a left hemiplegia. Such individuals often respond impulsively to questions, giving an impression of lower ability levels than they possess, or give occasionally bizarre responses to personality assessment measures indicative of impaired reality testing. With left hemisphere dysfunction, in addition to language impairments, individuals are likely to be much more uncertain and tentative, in what neurologists refer to as a "catastrophic reaction". An individual with left hemisphere problems following a stroke, for example, is likely to require a great deal of reassurance and encouragement, and to suffer from depression and feelings of helplessness. Such individuals are often doubtful of their own abilities, and may be reluctant to respond to questions when they are unsure of the answer. As a result, these persons may give an impression of greater mental impairment than they actually suffer.

In milder forms of lateralized cerebral asymmetry, such as might be apparent in learning disabled children, right hemisphere deficient individuals are more likely to appear careless and uneven in their application of attention to a task, and be comparatively poor in monitoring their own behavior (Hanson and Voeller 1982). Left hemisphere deficient individuals are often seen as lacking initiative, perhaps being too compulsive, and having difficulty adjusting to changing work situations. The behavioral differences associated with cerebral hemispheric functional asymmetries tend to be especially pronounced among individuals who have had neurologically mediated learning problems of a longstanding duration, probably reflecting the individual's attempts to deal with their selective cognitive processing weaknesses. The child who always has experienced difficulty dealing with such right hemisphere dependent tasks as picture puzzles, fine eye-hand coordination tasks, and spatial orientation, for example, is more likely to attempt to use language or other left hemisphere mediated abilities to solve problems, while the child with chronic language problems may find greater satisfaction in dealing with activities by a direct behavior approach rather than discussion.

Motor Facility

In addition to general intellectual and specific information processing deficits which may be apparent in learning disabled children, some persons in the LD population may exhibit signs of specific motor impairment. One type of motor deficit, dyspraxia, is defined as impaired ability to perform voluntary movement in absence of paralysis (Gardner, 1975). Dyspraxias may be exhibited in many different ways, such as ideational dyspraxia, in which the individual is unable to perform complex acts, such as dressing; or constructional dyspraxia, in which one has difficulty assembling pieces into a meaningful whole (Hécaen 1981).

The cells in the motor region of the cortex, known as the Betz cells, are among the largest of all neurons. Because of the large size of these upper motor neurons, they have high demands for oxygen in order to remain robust and functioning well. When oxygen flow to the brain is impaired, perhaps due to a long labor or a difficult birth, the Betz cells are the most vulnerable because of their extensive oxygen requirements. As a result, motor neurons may be damaged in some LD children, resulting in behavioral characteristics such as clumsiness, poor fine motor control, and constructional apraxia.

Various neuropsychological tests have been developed to identify the existence of discrete types of motor impairment, including rapid fine movement tasks such as finger oscillation (Reitan and Davison 1974) and the Purdue Pegboard Test (Purdue Research Foundation 1948) or measures of constructional apraxia such as the Developmental Test of Visual Motor Integration (Beery 1967) or the Benton Visual Retention Test (Benton 1974). Such measures can identify the presence of specific neuropsychological deficits in order to assist in educational and vocational planning.

The presence of specific motoric deficits is of relevance to parents, educators, and, especially, vocational planners who wish to maximize children's potential. Very young learning disabled children who exhibit fine motor deficits may display specific inefficiency in acquiring such self-care skills as buttoning, tying, and pouring. As such children mature somewhat, the presence of disability may be much less striking, but nevertheless it is still a factor. In middle school years when athletics begin to represent an important area for mastery, dyspraxic children may be unable to compete successfully. Written assignments may place unusual stress on such children, as well, and alternative response modes, such as typing, may be helpful.

The relevance of specific learning disabilities of motor functioning for vocational planning relates to the matching of job requirements to requisite skills. Children with neuropsychological deficits such as constructional apraxia would be ill-suited for such jobs which place a heavy emphasis on such abilities, like drafting. Similarly, careers which require such worker traits as rapid manipulative ability — assembler or machinist — probably would not be appropriate for learning disabled children who have deficits in such areas.

IMPLICATIONS OF NEUROPSYCHOLOGICAL TEST DATA FOR VOCATIONAL PLANNING

In spite of our most profound desires, all persons are not created equal. Some children have pervasive learning disabilities requiring years of painful adjustment, while other children appear to learn effortlessly. Recognition of neuropsychological deficits in learning disabled children, and appropriate matching of instruction strategies and vocational counseling, appears to be the most responsible course of action possible. In contrast, steadfast denial of the presence of identified neuropsychological limitations, when coupled with Pollyannish belief that sufficient motivation, drill, or desire will "remediate" the problem, represents an insidious disregard for children's feelings and genuine self-worth.

In a comprehensive review of aptitude-treatment studies in which neuropsychological models were used as the basis of identifying aptitudes, Hartlage and Telzrow (in press) reported consistent findings that educational intervention which utilized the existing neuropsychological strengths were more likely to produce favorable outcomes. In contrast, educational programs which relied upon a remediation of deficits approach were reported to demonstrate an increased incidence of frustration, as well as limited achievement gains.

Vocational planning, it has been said, begins long before children enter school. Observing parents and other adults at work, childhood play, and television and books all represent important sources of information about career options for young children. For normal as well as learning disabled children, parents are important resources for helping young people evaluate vocational options in light of their personal strengths and weaknesses. This process continues as the child progresses through the educational system, with increasing narrowing of the focus, so that over time fewer and fewer vocational options are within the student's consideration. As the student matures, careers which depend upon requisite skills not within his or her repertoire fall out of the pool for consideration.

At various steps during the student's educational program, formal evaluation might be utilized to help identify vocational interests as well as personal aptitudes and possible neuropsychological deficits. As the student progresses from grade to grade, the screen used to sort job options becomes progressively finer, so that careers thought possible at age ten might be eliminated at age sixteen, when it is apparent the student does not possess the interest or skills required. Simultaneously, the pool of all available occupations narrows, so the student's job sort becomes increasingly more concentrated. More detailed examples of how this model might operate in light of specific learning disabilities are provided in the following paragraphs.

Learning disabilities involving language (the dysphasias), can include receptive, expressive, or both modalities. A special type of language disorder, dyslexia, refers to a condition in which reading is uniquely impaired, although there need not be any impairment in comprehending spoken language. The academic correlates of these specific impairments, even when they occur in isolation, often go well beyond what might be attributable to the isolated learning disability. The individual with chronic reading disability will typically have difficulty with most school subjects which have test questions or homework assignments requiring reading, and will not uncommonly fall progressively farther behind in general fund of information, vocabulary, and other areas which normally depend on reading for continued mental progress. Such a learning disability, while educationally very handicapping, need not present too formidable a barrier to vocational habilitation, provided the individual possesses other work related abilities which can be applied to job titles wherein reading sophistication is not required. For such an individual, relating actual reading skill to the GED requirements of given jobs can normally identify a fairly wide range of vocational options, at least in the lower skill level job families. It is at this point that neuropsychological assessment can play a most useful role, since such assessment can fairly readily identify the specific (dyslexic) component of more widespread prior school difficulties.

For individuals with more pervasive dysphasic problems involving both receptive and expressive language processing disabilities, planning needs to take into account both training and placement considerations. Training for such individuals generally needs to focus on the more intact visuo spatial modalities, where pictorial representation, "hands-on" training, and repetition will be more effective than lecturing or similar approaches to instruction. With respect to job placement, such individuals tend to have better long term vocational prognoses in jobs wherein their comparatively strong visuo spatial skills can be brought to bear. Depending on the individual's mental ability, and the range of education feasible, individuals with language-based learning disabilities but comparatively good right cerebral hemisphere mediated abilities are more likely to do best in jobs utilizing strengths, such as assembler, inspector, tool and die maker, skilled trades, drafting, engineering, and, if the individual is quite bright, specialized fields like surgery.

Individuals with dyspraxias, reflected in poor eye-hand coordination or spatial problems, profit from job preparation in which instruction focuses on language-based sequential instruction emphasing the "why," rather than reliance on more visual aids. Placement can focus on work families wherein relatively better language skills can be the mainstay of successful job performance, and jobs where fine visual-motor performance is required can likewise be avoided. For the individual with better language skills and learning disabilities involving visuo-spatial abilities, jobs like sales, clerking, technical writing, teaching, and, if the individual is quite bright, psychiatry, represent jobs wherein comparative strengths can be brought to bear on meeting work requirements.

The focus on comparative strengths may well be the hallmark of successful rehabilitation or habilitation planning for individuals with learning disabilities. A learning disability which has not responded to twelve years of educators' attempts at remediation is not a good candidate for a "quick fix" by some job training program aimed at overcoming a chronic skill deficit based on underlying neurological dysfunction. Rather, by focusing attention on those things the student does well, and building on that individual's unique set of aptitudes and strengths, as revealed by careful neuropsychological assessment, the student's job potential can be maximized in such a way as to help match vocationally relevant assets to the world of work.

REFERENCES

Bannatyne, A. "The Spatially Competent LD Child." *Academic Therapy* 14, no. 2 (1978): 133–155.

Beery, K. E. *Developmental Test of Visual-Motor Integration: Manual.* Chicago, Ill.: Follet, 1967.

Benton, A. L. *The Revised Visual Retention Test,* 4th Ed. New York: The Psychological Corporation, 1974.

Boder, E. "Developmental Dyslexia: Prevailing Diagnostic Concepts and a new Diagnostic Approach." In H. R. Myklebust, ed., *Progress in Learning Disabilities.* Vol. 2. New York: Grune & Stratton, 1971.

Boder, E., and S. Jarrico. *The Boder Test of Reading-Spelling Patterns — Manual.* New York: Grune & Stratton, 1982.

Bogen, J. E. "Some Educational Implications of Hemispheric Specialization. "In M. C. Wittrock, ed., *The Human Brain.* Englewood Cliffs, N.J.: Prentice-Hall, 1977.

Buda, F. B. *The Neurology of Developmental Disabilities.* Springfield, Ill.: Charles C. Thomas, 1981.

Chi, J., E. Dooling, and F. Gilles. "Gyral Development of the Human Brain." *Annals of Neurology* 1, no. 1 (1977): 88–93.

Elliott, M. "Quantitative Evaluation Procedures for Learning Disabilities." *Journal of Learning Disabilities* 14 (1981): 84–87.

Galaburda, A. M., M. LeMay, T. L. Kemper, and N. Geschwind. "Right-Left Asymmetries in the Brain." *Science* 199 (1978): 852–856.

Gardner, E. *Fundamentals of Neurology.* Philadelphia: Saunders, 1975.

Geschwind, N. "Asymmetries of the Brain: New Developments." *Bulletin of the Orton Society* 29 (1979): 67–73.

Geschwind, N., and W. Levitsky. "Human Brain, Left-Right Asymmetries in Temporal Speech Region." *Science* 161 (1968): 186–187.

Hanson, J., and K. K. S. Voeller. "The Effect of Right Cerebral Dysfunction on the Ability of Young Children to Read the Affectual States of Others and

Its Implications for Learning Disabled and Behaviorally Disordered Children." *The Midwest Regional Conference on Neuropsychological Aspects of Learning Disabilities.* Toledo, Ohio, 1982.

Hartlage, L. C. "Management of Common Clinical Problems: Learning Disabilities." *School Related Health Care.* Ross Laboratories Monograph #9 (1979): 28–33.

_____. "Neuropsychological Assessment Techniques." In C. R. Reynolds and T. Gutkin, eds., *Handbook of School Psychology.* New York: Wiley, 1981.

Hartlage, L. C., and P. L. Hartlage. "Neuropsychological Principles and Learning Disabilities." In L. Tarnapol and M. Tarnapol, eds., *Brain Function and Reading Disabilities.* Baltimore: University Park Press, 1977.

Hartlage, L. C., and P. L. Hartlage. "Psychological Testing in Neurological Diagnosis." In J. R. Youmans, ed., *Neurological Surgery,* 2nd ed. New York: Saunders, 1982.

Hartlage, L. C., and C. F. Telzrow. "The Neuropsychological Bases of Educational Intervention." *Journal of Learning Disabilities,* in press.

Hartlage, L. C., C. F. Telzrow, N. A. DeFilippis, J. B. Shaw, and M. Noonan. "Personality Correlates of Functional Cerebral Asymmetry in Preschool Children." *Clinical Neuropsychology* 5, no. 1 (1983): 14–15.

Hécaen, H. "Apraxias." In S. B. Filskov and T. J. Boll, eds., *Handbook of Clinical Neuropsychology.* New York: Wiley, 1981.

Lechtenberg, R. The Psychiatrist's Guide to Diseases of the Nervous System. New York: Wiley, 1982.

Levy, J. "Cerebral Asymmetries as Manifested in Split-Brain Man." In M. Kinsbourne and W. L. Smith, eds., *Hemispheric Disconnection and Cerebral Function.* Springfield, Ill.: Charles C. Thomas, 1974.

Levy, J. "Cerebral Asymmetry and the Psychology of Man." In M.C. Wittrock, ed., *The Brain and Psychology.* New York: Academic Press, 1980.

Levy, J., and J. M. Levy. "Human Lateralization from Head to Foot: Sex-Related Factors." *Science* 200, no. 16 (1978): 1291–1292.

Marcel, T., L. Katz, and M. Smith. "Laterality and Reading Proficiency." *Neuropsychologia* 12 (1974): 131–139.

Meisels, S. J., and N. J. Anastasiow. "The Risks of Prediction: Relationships between Etiology, Handicapping Conditions, and Developmental Outcomes." In S. Moore and C. Cooper, eds., *The Young Child: Reviews of Research,* Vol. 3. Washington, D.C.: National Association for the Education of Young Children, 1980.

Nebes, R. D. "Dominance of the Minor Hemisphere, in Commissuratomized Man for the Perception of Part-Whole Relationships." In M. Kinsbourne and W. L. Smith, eds., *Hemispheric Disconnection and Cerebral Function.* Springfield, Ill.: Charles C. Thomas, 1974.

Nebes, R. D. "Man's So-called Minor Hemisphere." In M. C. Wittrock, ed., *The Human Brain.* Englewood Cliffs, N.J.: Prentice-Hall, 1977.

Purdue Research Foundation. *Examiner's Manual for the Purdue Pegboard.* Chicago: Science Research Associates, 1948.

Reitan, R. M., and L. A. Davison, eds. *Clinical Neuropsychology: Current Status and Applications.* Washington, D.C.: Winston & Sons, 1974.

Reynolds, C. R. "The Fallacy of 'Two Years Below Grade Level for Age' as a Diagnostic Criterion for Reading Disabilities." *Journal of School Psychology* 19 (1981): 350–358.

Shepard, L. "An Evaluation of the Regression Discrepancy Method for Identifying Children with Learning Disabilities." *The Journal of Special Education* 14 (1980): 79–91.

Telzrow, C. F., E. Century, C. Redmond, B. Whittaker, and B. Zimmerman. "The Boder Test: Neuropsychological and Demographic Features of Dyslexic Subtypes." *Psychology in the Schools,* in press.

Witelson, S. F., and W. Pallie. "Left Hemisphere Specialization for Language in the Newborn." *Brain* 96 (1973): 641–646.

PROGRAMS FOR ADOLESCENTS

13

Denver Academy
A Program for Learning Disabled Adolescents

Paul D. Knott and Stephan D. Tattum

Denver Academy was founded in 1972 as a private school specializing in the education of adolescents (ages 12–18) with learning disabilities. The Academy has a few classes for pre-adolescent children but is known mainly for its work with LD adolescents. Students must be of at least average intelligence, exhibit identifiable learning disabilities, but not exhibit *primary* emotional/social disturbance. Prior to admittance, students typically have shown a dramatic decline in self-esteem, a significant discrepancy between aptitude and achievement, and often a prior history of "acting-out."

In the early 1970s it was still common to hear professionals comment that "unless you get to the LD child by the time he is 10 or 11, it's a lost cause." Our experience in working with LD adolescents has been highly positive and in dramatic contrast to the above attitude. To be sure, there are important differences in the successful education of LD adolescents versus pre-adolescents. We hope to point out some of these differences in this paper. Adolescents place great demands on teachers both in terms of discipline and the much broader spectrum of curriculum that must be provided beyond the "basics." A normal class at the Academy (ten students) is run by a master teacher assisted either by an aide or teacher intern. The master teacher is the heart and soul of our program. We learned many years ago that new teachers, even if well credentialed, simply could not step into our program and perform at the high level of quality established by our beginning nucleus of faculty. We thus began our teacher intern program. All new faculty must go through a minimum two years of on-the-job training that emphasizes classroom structure and management, student counseling and discipline techniques, acquisition of multi-sensory teaching techniques across all subjects, and proper use of our individualization methods in language and math. Interns observe master teachers at work and review our privately developed library of video tapes that addresses in detail all the above areas. Interns are slowly weaned from small, very specific responsibilities to large ones. At each step interns are observed and later critiqued in private by a master teacher; the intern must demonstrate competence in all areas before being promoted. Teacher training has thus become a major focus of Denver Academy. We have provided training programs for public and private schools outside of Colorado and established two model LD schools in Canada. Although our model of teacher training is not a major focus of this article, it is crucial to note this factor since it is the foundation of our program.

In the first section of this paper the Academy's language program will be outlined. In the second section our approach to structure and discipline will be spotlighted. In the final section follow-up data on former students will be presented.

LANGUAGE PROGRAM

The Academy's language program reflects a strong emphasis on utilizing all available research as a beacon light for programatic considerations. We classify students within five major diagnostic prescriptive categories. These classifications are meant for teacher use only as a starting point in program determination; the labels are simplistic and not all inclusive. There are two dimensions we feel most clearly differentiate LD adolescents. The first is the ability to learn *inductively,* i.e., the skill of picking up the rules of language without direction instruction (Enfield 1982). Our more severe LD students are not inductive learners. They cannot, for example, pick out grapho-phonemic regularities from a language experience lesson. The students' inductive abilities are assessed by teachers during the first month of school. The second dimension is demonstrated by difficulty on visual aptitude tests. Deficits of revisualization for words are demonstrated on the Monroe aptitude tests, Slingerland tests, handwriting samples, informal written paragraphs, and spelling and reading tests. The following classifications help formulate practical remedial strategies based on student strengths.

Dyslexic

These students exhibit virtually no inductive ability and very little visual memory for words. Reading and spelling are significantly below grade level (0–3.5 at time of admission). These students must be taught directly the structure and science of language. A great deal of drill work is necessary stressing phonetic regularities in both reading and spelling. A strong systematic phonics program such as Orton-Gillingham works best with this group.

Secondary Language Problem (SL)

These students show slightly more inductive ability than Dyslexics and reading is slightly more fluid (grade 1.5–3.5). Spelling and writing are very poor (1.5–3.5). Grade levels may be similar to Dyslexics but these students can more quickly acquire the rules of language with less drill. SLs benefit most from a systematic linguistic text such as Bloomfield's *Let's Read* or a phonetic series such as *Mott*. Little if any drill work in blending or flashcards for reading is required although drill is needed in the phonetic regularities of spelling (Hanna 1971).

Educationally Handicapped (EH)

These students show fairly good inductive abilities; they can pick out many of the rules of language without direction instruction. They often have visual memory abilities slightly below normal population. Typically, these students will be one–two years below grade level in reading and two–three years below grade level in spelling. In all likelihood they would never have required our services if they had earlier been taught via a structured developmental approach to language skills. Such students respond much better to intrinsic phonics instruction rather than systematic phonics (Chall, 1967; Spache, 1981). Our accent is to use good literature for reading. We teach structural analysis (6 syllable and two major syllable division rules) as opposed to work with phonemes. Much time is also devoted to work with context. The student is taught to utilize the first syllable of the word in combination with context in predicting an unfamiliar word. Spelling is developed by emphasizing the most important generalizations and rules in combination with work on the Dolch (1955) 2,000 spelling word list. Since these students have some visual memory abilities, we utilize the self-corrected pre-test and study techniques indicated by Loomer (1978).

Dysphonetic (Boder 1971)

These students may or may not have inductive skills. Their visual memory is frequently excellent, but auditory skills such as blending and synthesis are deficit. They can range from 0–12 grade level in reading and frequently have associated comprehension problems. If their inductive skills are intact, a whole language method as suggested by Smith (1978) in combination with language experience is most effective. If, however, as frequently occurs in the LD population, more direct instruction is needed then the Fernald method is the better approach. As the student develops his reading abilities a basal or good literature text is utilized for instruction. The use of context and structured analysis, similar to the EH program advocated above, is utilized for word attack skills. Spelling is primarily visual and kinesthetic using either the Fernald method or suggestions by Loomer (1978). The major spelling rules as indicated by Loomer are taught.

Attentional Deficits (AD)

These students are often very inductive and some may fit under Daniel's (1983) label of "gifted LD." These are bright students who lack sophisticated vocabularies, are slow in speed of reaction and rigid in their approach to problems. Many show the characteristics of "hyperactive" students as classified by Tant and Douglas (1982): they are overly concrete and their attentional deficits prevent them from acquiring effective problem solving strategies. Although word recognition is not a problem, they often experience difficulties with comprehension due to attentional and organizational deficits. As adolescents these students are not as overtly hyperactive as when they were younger, but they still exhibit residual effects that impede learning. We tend to agree with Tant and Douglas (1982) that "LD" and "hyperactive" represent somewhat different diagnostic categories. Reading, generally above 6th grade level, is approached through the whole language method (Smith 1978). Some work on word attack is directed toward use of context and structural analysis, but the primary emphasis is on meaning. Some class time is spent reading high interest novels. The spelling program is based totally on Loomer's (1978) research in that a list of 675 frequently misspelled words is taught using self-corrected pretest and study techniques. The few spelling rules that work for normals are also taught with this group (Loomer 1978).

Group assignments by diagnostic category also take into account such factors as the student's age and maturity, his need for structure, and his functional grade level in basic academic skills. Although the Dysphonetic student is sometimes placed mainly with EH students, he receives more seatwork and one-to-one work in the use of context than the EH student who requires more work with structural analysis. All diagnostic placements are reassessed about once/month in accordance with teachers' judgments.

As summarized in Figure 13.1 it has been our experience that the major considerations in successful language placement for LD adolescents are (a) the degree to which the student can learn inductively the rules of language and (b) his visual memory aptitude.

Figure 13.1. Five Diagnostic Categories of LD Adolescents as Defined by Inductive vs. Non-Inductive and Visual Memory Aptitude.*

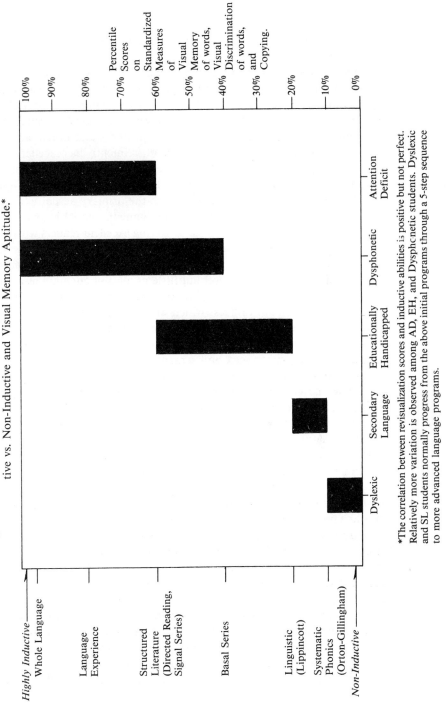

*The correlation between revisualization scores and inductive abilities is positive but not perfect. Relatively more variation is observed among AD, EH, and Dysphonetic students. Dyslexic and SL students normally progress from the above initial programs through a 5-step sequence to more advanced language programs.

Applications of Theory and Research

The theoretical basis of our approach is guided by the insights of the psycholinguistic model of reading. Our goal is to have students obtain meaning from print. Students must bring into play semantic, syntactical and grapho-phonemic knowledge in order to become sophisticated readers. Students enter our program with various competences and potentialities in all three areas. For example, the AD student frequently has excellent word attack skills (grapho-phonemic knowledge) and a good feel for syntax, but semantic flexibility is underdeveloped. Methodologies ascribed to Smith (1978) are very helpful with such students: the primary accent is reading for meaning. We depart from the psycholinguistic model in that we do not apply its inferences, gained from observing excellent readers with good inductive abilities, to students who have little or no inductive skills, e.g., Dyslexic and SL problems. Dyslexic adolescents frequently have semantic and syntactical skills at age level but little grapho-phonemic knowledge. They cannot bring their language into play because they cannot break the code of print; it is hard to guess which word is predictable from the context when one has been guessing at every word one comes across. Our stress then is on developing phonic and structural analysis skills to enable them to use their adequate syntax and semantics.

The five diagnostic labels serve as guidelines for primary instructional approaches developed through the context of an overall language program. All students receive one-to-one tutoring in the *Reading for Understanding Program* (Thurstone 1978). This program stresses predictability of thought patterns as well as inferential abilities. We modify the program according to the suggestions of Ansara (1976): the student reads a small paragraph and then fills in the last phrases to complete the paragraph. He first writes down what he thinks is appropriate before picking one of the four responses given by the publisher. Semantic and syntactical correspondence can then be dealt with effectively: does the student follow the thought patterns (semantic knowledge) as well as complete the paragraph with correct grammar (syntax)? The student has to read for meaning to complete this exercise. We use the *Specific Skills* series for individual problems in comprehension. Though we believe comprehension problems are due greatly to poor organization of information, we feel direct work on specific problems is helpful emphasizing inferences and main idea books. Context (Cloze) books are especially helpful for Dysphonetics or students relying totally on structural analysis for word attack.

A popular aspect of our program is a modification of *Hooked on Books* (Fader 1981) and independent reading (Spache 1977; Barbe 1975).

Students select books to read mainly on their own time. These books have summaries and questions attached to enable the teacher to test the student's comprehension. We depart from uninterrupted silent reading by having private 6 to 10 minute conferences with students. This individual conference is often the most diagnostically valuable portion of our reading program. Students typically look forward to the conference that starts with two or more minutes of oral reading or directed silent reading, depending on the student's reading level. Generally, Dyslexics and SLs receive more work on vocabulary and oral, choral and repeated readings. The teacher develops a folder on each student that contains an oral reading checklist, troublesome words, comprehension deficits, number of pages read since last conference, comprehension questions and plot summaries (Barbe 1975). Conferences end with vocabulary and comprehension reviews.

An extrinsic system of motivation accompanies this program. A student who completes successfully five books receives gratis a Denver Academy blue T-shirt. A student who reads ten books receives a green shirt, 15 books a brown shirt, and twenty books a black shirt (thus completing the corollary to the time proven belt system of the martial arts). Normally, the book is material a student could reasonably read in 2½ weeks. For a Dyslexic, this may mean a 75-page book. An AD may need to read 200 pages for a book. The exciting part of this program is that it works. Students who refused to read are now reading books for leisure. Intrinsic reinforcement is supplementing extrinsic reinforcement. We also allow students in the five book club to buy a letterman's sweater and those in the ten book club to buy a letterman's coat. The signal to the students: reading success is as highly valued as athletic success.

The spelling segment of our program has been alluded to under each diagnostic category. Dyslexics and SLs receive a great deal of training in sound symbol relationships. We teach regular spelling as demonstrated by Hanna (1971) and practical applications as developed by Cox (1980). These students are also taught rules for adding suffixes to base words as well as the major generalizations such as when to use the graphemes *tch* or *ch*. The EH and Dysphonetic groups are given the Structured Spelling Test (Tattum 1982) that pinpoints specific weaknesses in the various areas mentioned above. There is less drill on sound symbol relationships and more work on rules and generalizations. In addition, these groups study a revised edition of the Dolch words for spelling (1955). They receive self-corrected pre-tests on Mondays and post-tests on Fridays. Missed words are studied using a modification of the Fernald Method. AD students review suffix rules, then study a list of 675 "spelling demons" we have assembled. The common thread that runs through all five spelling programs is overlearning of frequently misspelled words using the modified Fernald method. All teachers emphasize words missed in compositions, for these are the words in the child's natural language.

All spelling generalizations and sound symbol relationships are reinforced in composition periods. During proof reading students underline every word with a suffix and make sure they have applied appropriate rules. When a student is writing a story and does not know a word, we ask him to write what he knows and draw a line for the rest of the word (mis_____ for mistake). We initially help him with spelling during proof reading but eventually have him look up the word in a dictionary and make his own spelling cards. We want the student to be self-sufficient. Notice that we do not interrupt the natural flow of writing with the spelling problem. Our essential goal is that students convey their thoughts in a coherent fashion on paper. Each composition class generally starts with 10 minutes of work on sentence building or sentence combining as advised by Straw (1981). Poor writers receive much more work on building sentences. Parts of speech are mentioned but not stressed as in conventional grammar class. Students then spend 20–30 minutes a day on writing. We alternate units on creative writing and the essay. Creative writing is predicated on where the child falls on the Johnson and Myklebust sequence (1967). Can he only describe a picture (concrete description), infer what might be happening (concrete imagination), add time (abstract description), or can he follow a complete story line with introduction, rising action, climax and conclusion (abstract imagination)? The essay starts with the development of topic sentences and supporting ideas. The students learn to write a good paragraph on topics they generate (Graves 1982). We eventually move to comparison and contrast essays and, finally, research papers. In the last ten minutes students read their compositions while classmembers comment on them. Any common problems in punctuation, capitalization or usage can be dealt with at this time or during the first ten minutes of class in lieu of sentence work.

It should be noted that our math program is not predicated on the above diagnostic labels. A Dyslexic student may be an excellent math student with no manifestation of Dyscalculia. Language problems do not always interfere with computation skills but often affect word problems. All adolescent students move through individualized programs as recommended by our math coordinator (Loan 1982). Students with severe problems receive remedial work using Montessori techniques. Math fact tests are given weekly and students are given cards to study troublesome facts. We use the *Addison-Wesley Program for Reluctant Learners* (Foley 1982) that allows students to move at their own pace. We form new math groups daily depending on problems students are presenting. Once the student demonstrates a high level of competency in basic math skills, he is placed in consumer math and/or algebra classes.

The final aspect of our program is integration: all language skills are reinforced in our Science, History and Social Science courses. We emphasize the need to change modalities during these lessons. All classes involve auditory (oral presentations, discussions), visual (overheads, filmstrips, pictures, readings) and kinesthetic (note-taking, drawing, roleplaying, lab work) processes with lectures lasting twenty minutes maximum. All students are taught notetaking skills using a systematic six step approach (Tattum, 1983) that guides the student from filling in phrases on a ditto to outlining a spontaneous oral lecture. Metacognitive processes (Flavell 1977; Reid 1981) are emphasized in order to involve our students more actively in learning. We teach strategies that aid in clustering and retaining information. For example, reading skills are reinforced through the curriculum: skimming is utilized as a vehicle for review and students are asked to guess which essay questions they will likely be asked regarding the lesson. Preview techniques are utilized in dealing with the next day's lessons. Essay questions require the students to use techniques taught in composition classes. The emphasis is on teaching students how to transfer their skills to a more conventional classroom setting.

The Academy thus deals with the language problems of LD adolescents through a combination of group and individual work with the primary guidelines being the student's inductive abilities and visual memory aptitude. All students are impressed with the importance of reading for meaning. Even the Dyslexic who receives Orton-Gillingham training also receives work on language experience, especially in beginning stages. As Jansky (1981) found with first graders, students must realize the correspondence between speech and reading. In addition, daily work on listening comprehension is conducted via oral reading to students from good books interwoven with questions and predictions. The stress on meaning is further reinforced even when the student is using phonics; he is asked: does that make sense? At the same time, we are concerned that our better readers are aware of the graphophonemic aspects of words in combination with their context and meaning. Our objective then, is to develop independent, well rounded readers who not only comprehend well, but enjoy reading. We feel our program usually accomplishes this objective.

STRUCTURE AND DISCIPLINE

It has been our experience that all success with LD adolescents begins with appropriate *structure*. We refer to our system as "positive structure." Discipline is a major component of positive structure since it refers to specific procedures used for teaching the student alternatives to misbehavior. Structure refers to the overall set-up of the classroom, school rules, and interactional techniques between teachers and students. *Positive structure* is our label for our total system of teacher and school expectations and the ways in which these expectations are implemented with students.

Cruickshank (1977) has stated with respect to the LD child: "His techniques of adjustment are so fragmentary that to place him in a permissive environment only serves to heighten his tensions and to increase and reinforce his feelings of insecurity and inadequacy" (p. 146). Cruickshank may have been thinking mainly of younger children, but in our experience his statement is crucially appropriate for LD adolescents. In working with adolescents, however, we do not stress the physical environment as in the use of carrels. Most adolescents find carrels to be demeaning; they respond better to a conventionally arranged classroom. We do, however, stress the full utilization of program and teacher structure. Cruickshank notes that a well-structured program can be achieved through "sheer dint of excellent programming and total devotion to the logical aspects of a good developmental experience for children" (p. 148). In working with adolescents we find that particular forms of programmatic structure and teacher training are essential to our successes.

When we first began working with adolescents we investigated the psychological literature on the effects of punishment and rewards on behavior. This research was combined with our knowledge of learning disabilities and good school practices in general so as to develop our system of *positive structure*. We wanted to develop a system that incorporated the following features. First, the system must address the specific misbehavior, not the personality or character of the student. Second, the system must be essentially simple and relatively easy to teach to all teachers and support personnel. Third, the act of punishment itself should occur in a swift and sure manner. Fourth, the teacher should be able to return quickly to a positive mode of interaction with the student soon after the act of punishment; the punishment itself should be as short and to the point as possible. Fifth, the system should allow the teacher to avoid the gradual build up of frustration and hostility toward the student that results in a fit of anger; the technique should thus allow the teacher to intervene early in the process and have considerable control over the situation. Sixth, the system should thus encourage the teacher to head off most problems before they become major, while at the same time providing the teacher with a technique to utilize if his authority is challenged. Seventh, a system was required that would encourage the teacher to be positive toward students the vast bulk of time and thus to serve as a positive role model for students.

Eighth, the system should encourage the student to work toward a greater degree of freedom from structure and increased responsibilities. Ninth, we wanted to attain these goals without using M & M approaches, overt token systems, etc. We thus wanted to utilize naturalistic rewards and punishments that would be more readily internalized by students and more readily generalized to other situations.

Discipline

Probably the strongest finding in current research on effective vs noneffective schools is that effective teachers are able to maintain students *on task* most of the time (Tursman 1981). Our discipline system first evolved eleven years ago because we wanted to insure that all our teachers knew how to keep LD students on task. A group of LD adolescents, well versed in manipulation techniques and disruptive behavior, can quickly take over a classroom headed by a "regular" or inexperienced teacher. New teachers, fresh out of college, have rarely been taught a systematic approach to classroom management. We quickly discovered that a crucial concept to teach new teachers is that discipline is most effective when it is administered by a person the student perceives as being a warm and caring human being. If the teacher is perceived only as a strong disciplinarian then students, while being respectful, often will engage in passive/aggressive subterfuge toward the teacher. The strict disciplinarian is not as effective, over the long haul, as is the teacher who effectively combines firm discipline with a warm, humorous, reinforcing approach to students. This is the idea — the combination of *positiveness with firmness* — that we constantly strive to attain.

The reader is forewarned (1) that our system may sound unusual on paper but, upon viewing, its positive impact on students is obvious and (2) that although our system is simple in principle its successful application is dependent on extensive teacher training.

First, all teachers are trained to scan their rooms constantly. Less experienced teachers have a tendency to fixate on the task at hand and lose sight of what is going on throughout the classroom. A disturbance "suddenly" erupts when in reality it has been building for several moments while the teacher has been working on a specific project with other students. Teachers are taught that in their scanning they should intervene immediately at the first sign of a disturbance. New teachers often feel that "if I ignore that small bit of misbehavior, it may go away." Rarely is this the case with LD adolescents. Failure to respond by the teacher is often seen as an invitation to repeat and/or intensify the misbehavior. Dependent upon the form of misbehavior, teachers are taught either (a) give the student an immediate warning or (b) immediately check the student's level of work to determine if it is at his frustrational level and thus needs to be modified downward accordingly.

Second, if the student violates his first warning, which is administered in a firm but calm voice, he may be given a second warning (dependent on circumstances), but no more. Either on the second or third violation, the teacher is taught to discipline the misbehavior by using our modification of time-out procedure. The student is told to "take that behavior to the wall." The student must go and stand facing the wall at a designated spot in the room. The teacher makes sure that the student stands nose and toes against the wall with arms fully extended over his head with the palms of the hands also touching the wall. We know that after about two minutes upper arms and shoulders undergo muscle fatigue that quickly translates into physical discomfort. After the student has been at the wall 3–5 minutes the teachers turns away from his ongoing instruction with the other students and quickly asks the youngster why he is at the wall. If the student responds with an appropriate and polite response, he is told to retake his seat and return immediately to work. The teacher then quickly returns to a normal mode of interaction with the student. If, however, the student is inappropriate at the wall, or tries to argue with the teacher about the act of discipline, or his tone is "sassy," then he is told he must stay at the wall until his behavior and attitude are appropriate.

This procedure typically allows the teacher to discipline without physically touching the student. It also provides the teacher with ultimate authority so that he or she is not dependent on the old ruse of "if you keep that up I'm going to send you to the principal." If a student refuses to go to the wall then the teacher immediately escorts him to the wall with no further verbalizations. If necessary, the teacher will physically restrain the student, with his arms around the student's body, and hold him to the wall. Such incidents are thankfully rare, and when they occur the teacher can count on almost immediate help from a second teacher. The social norm has been established over the years that at the Academy one goes quietly when told. This norm has been partly attained by mixing new with experienced students in each classroom. Older students lead the way by demonstrating correct "at the wall" technique to newer students. Out of 170 students, we now average 3–6 physical restraints, schoolwide, in an academic year. Many of our master teachers have not had to restrain a student in years. Improved methods of teacher training are mainly responsible for this positive change.

One of the more interesting features of the above technique is how its usage declines during the school year. By spring most teachers use the wall an average of only two times/week. In the first few weeks of the fall the average is two-three times per day. This average begins to drop off in October with the low average rate of two incidents per week usually attained shortly after Christmas break. Our master teachers acquire and project the attitude of "I am in control; I know what I'm doing; you can't get my goat; if you provoke a power struggle I'll win, but I'm reasonable." Our discipline techniques thus free the teacher to be positive with students the vast majority of time. This in turn results in a warm environment readily seen and felt in our classrooms.

Third, it is essential that when a student has completed his discipline he be returned fairly quickly to a positive mode of interaction with the teacher. Teachers are taught that for the first few minutes after a discipline they should treat the student in a normal manner. Before the end of the class period the teacher in some way, often indirectly, expresses his approval of the student as a person so that he is reminded that he is an "OK" kid even though the teacher had to discipline him. This expression may take the form of a squeeze of the student's shoulder as the teacher passes by or some other non-verbal communication. Teachers are drilled in the concept of never holding a grudge toward a student they have had to discipline. We wish to avoid falling into the trap of negative scanning whereby the teacher unconsciously begins to respond only to negative output and disregards the positive aspects of the student's behavior. Negative scanning is one of the more pernicious traps of interpersonal interaction and is all too easy to fall into. LD adolescents have often been caught up in negative scanning with the authority figures in their lives. It is crucial that they understand that an authority figure can discipline them and yet at the same time hold them in high regard as worthwhile human beings. Teachers are trained in the concept of "catching the child while he is doing good" so that there is a high frequency of positive stroking of students throughout the normal class period. The curriculum in each class is designed so the student works at his instructional level wherein he experiences a high frequency of successes. We try to structure all the variables so that what we call the "magic ratio" — the ratio of positive to negative feedback from teacher to student — is heavily loaded toward the positive.

Safety Valves

Whenever one is running a structured setting in which the teachers are strong authority figures, it is important to have safety valves whereby students can let off steam with the teacher or any aspect of the system. This factor has its special place in our program. For example, teachers never engage in argument with a youngster during the act of discipline itself. Verbalization by the teacher is then at a bare minimum. Many LD adolescents are past masters at out-verbalizing adults, sidetracking them, and altogether conning them out of effective action. Our motto with our teachers is "act, don't talk." While such a system is highly effective, teachers are bound to make mistakes, and students need to learn how to express complaints in a context of being taught how to problem solve rather than being passive-aggressive or manipulative. To this end, we run *values* classes three times a week. Though there is not space here to discuss our values curriculum in detail, the overall objective is use of the Socratic method to stimulate the student to think about his personal values, the meanings and implications thereof, to expose him to other major thought and values systems and to relate the above to his own mode of interaction with peers and authority figures. Most LD adolescents have difficulties in all the above areas. Values classes are sometimes used as "family time" during which students and teachers are in a circle and students may express any and all complaints in a non-punitive setting. The teacher takes note of complaints and if he, or the supervising master teacher, determines that he has acted in a non-justifiable manner, then the teacher is encouraged to apologize to the student and/or the classroom as a whole. It is important that students see authority figures as persons who can admit to mistakes and learn from them. Teachers also spend time every week doing one-on-one counseling with students. These sessions are confidential and provide the student with additional opportunities to express concerns and anxieties to their teachers. Active listening techniques are often used by teachers during these sessions. Through these avenues, students learn that they have conduits of communication to the teacher/authority figures. They are encouraged to use these conduits in an assertive, problem solving manner that the teacher models for the student.

Whereas our total school structure is too extensive a topic for this chapter, it is important to note (1) that all students are put to work as soon as they enter a classroom, (2) that except for informal periods, a student cannot speak unless acknowledged by the teacher as having first raised his hand and then only one student can speak at a time, and (3) that students must always address peers and teachers in a respectful, courteous manner; no put-downs are tolerated. The total structure for a new student is thus highly organized with virtually every moment organized for him. He learns quickly that although his teachers are very warm personalities they will not brook any breach of the structure. After the first few months of the program, however, students are reviewed to determine those that can move to more advanced stages. Our structure is designed so that as a student moves into more advanced work the structure is gradually lessened. As the student demonstrates that he has internalized the initial structure, and the reasoning behind it, he is advanced to higher rooms that are somewhat less structured than before. Typically, students spend between two and four academic years at the Academy. Our goal is for the student to obtain a high degree of self-discipline and responsibility by the time he leaves us. This goal is met in the overwhelming majority of cases. It is our experience that students do not learn responsibility and self-discipline nearly as well in permissive settings as they do in positive but structured environments wherein they can readily progress from more to less structure. Our emphasis on the *positive* aspects of our structure cannot be minimized since it is the overall positiveness that engenders *internalization* by students.

The final destination for about a third of our older adolescents is our College Prep track. Between 80 and 90 percent of the students in this program go directly to college after graduation from the Academy. Those students who have earned their way into the College Prep program are handled in a way that is hardly distinct from conventional college preparatory schools. Our prep program includes some on-going remedial instruction, but its curriculum, designed several years ago, is mainly along the lines discussed in the Paideia Proposal (Adler 1982).

A few years ago we had the opportunity to experiment with modifications of our positive structure so as to assist a large public school system that was having both discipline and racial problems (SADCU 1982). The program we implemented was apparently very successful as determined by an independent research agency (Maurer 1982). Incidents of school violence dropped precipitously while drop-out rates declined significantly as did tardy and absentee rates. Although our system of positive structure was designed for the LD adolescent, it has been our repeated experience that many of its components are very effective in conventional classrooms. Many of its features are congruent with the research that delineates the characteristics of effective versus noneffective schools. This research suggests that more effective schools are characterized by better discipline, more orderliness, and by teachers who are better able to keep students on task (Tursman 1981). These are all factors we have been refining for the last decade in our work with LD adolescents.

FOLLOW-UP DATA

Table 13.1 is a summary of a recently conducted study of 106 students who attended Denver Academy for at least two full academic years during

Table 13.1
Post-High School Performance
of Academy Students vs. Comparison Group

Comparison Items	Former Academy Students N = 106 Av. Age = 21.1 yrs.	Former Public School Students N = 46 Av. Age = 22.2 yrs.
% who attended college/university for one year	52	24
% currently attending college full time	39	11
% presently holding full time job	53	41
% presently holding part time job	4	20
% presently unemployed	4	28
% of those not attending college full time but functioning as independent adults	77	37

the ages of 13–18. It is our experience that a student must attend the Academy for a minimum two years in order for him to have a reasonable chance of long-term success. These students were randomly drawn from slightly more than 1,000 students the Academy has serviced over the last decade. The data were obtained through telephone and personal interviews, following a standardized format, with both former students and their parents.

Table 13.1 also shows comparable data obtained on a comparison group of 46 students. These students had been evaluated by our diagnostic staff and had met the criteria for acceptance into Denver Academy. These 46 students chose not to attend the Academy most often because they did not wish to be removed from their friends and/or transportation (bus routes) was a major problem. Finances were rarely the major obstacle since these 46 families were by and large of the same socioeconomic (S-E) standing as those who attended the Academy. All 46 students remained in public school wherein they received resource room help from an LD specialist while being for the most part mainstreamed. This is the most common approach to helping LD adolescents in Denver area schools.

Clearly, the data provided in Table 13.1 comprise a post hoc comparison. Although every attempt was made to rule out contaminating factors it must be noted that the comparison group is not a true control group.

As can be seen in Table 13.1, 52 percent of 106 former Academy students attended college for at least one year; 39 percent are still attending college, and most expect to complete their bachelor's degree. This statistic is interesting since the Academy accepts a near full range of learning disabilities and does not take only those who are clear college material. The number attending trade school is not reported due to its smallness, which is probably a reflection of the S-E status of this population. Of the 65 students not presently attending college, 56 hold full time jobs while another 4 have part-time jobs. Most heartening is that 50 of this group of 65 are functioning as independent adults. To meet this criterion both the former students and their parents had to agree that (a) he or she held a full time job, (b) lived apart from his parents, (c) paid his own bills and (d) was essentially an independent agent. It is clear from Table 13.1 that those students who chose to stay in the public school LD programs have not fared nearly as well as Academy students. Our comparison group shows many similarities to the patterns of difficulty exhibited by LD adults in a study by White, *et al.* (1982).

Most heartening of all were the spontaneous comments of nearly 90 percent of our former students and their parents: "Denver Academy changed my life," "He never could have made it otherwise," "The Academy gave me confidence for the first time," etc. Such comments, when made time after time, cannot be taken lightly. The above data, both objective and subjective, support our belief that the LD adolescent can exhibit significant positive growth if provided with an appropriate program.

REFERENCES

Adler, Mortimer. *Paideia Proposal: An Educational Manifesto.* New York: Macmillan, 1982.

Ansara, Alice. "Secondary Language Development and the Adolescent." Paper presented at Educator's Publishing Company Workshop, Oysterville, Mass., 1976.

Barbe, Walter B., and Jerry L. Barbe. *Personalized Reading Instruction: New Techniques That Increase Reading Skill and Comprehension.* New York: Parker, 1975.

Boder, Elena. "Developmental Dyslexia: A Diagnostic Screening Procedure Based on Three Characteristic Patterns of Reading and Spelling," *Learning Disorders* 4 (1971).

Chall, Jeanne S. *Learning to Read: The Great Debate.* New York: McGraw-Hill, 1967.

Cox, Aylett R. *Structures and Techniques: A Multisensory Teaching of Basic Language Skills.* Cambridge, Mass.: Educator Publishing Service, 1980.

Cruickshank, William. *Learning Disabilities in Home, School and Community.* Syracuse: Syracuse University Press, 1977.

Daniels, Paul R. *Teaching the Gifted/Learning Disabled Child.* Rockville, Md.: Aspen, 1983.

Dolch, Edward W. *The 2000 Commonest Words for Spelling.* Champaign, Ill.: Garrard, 1955.

Enfield, Mary Lee. "An Alternative Approach to Teaching Reading Comprehension to Children/Adolescents With Language Learning Disabilities." Paper presented at the Annual Conference of the Orton Society, Baltimore, Md., 1982.

Fader, Daniel. *The New Hooked on Books.* New York: Berkley Books, 1981.

Flavell, John H. *Cognitive Development.* Englewood Cliffs, N.J.: Prentice-Hall, 1977.

Foley, Jack, and others. *Building Math Skills: An Individual Approach.* Menlo Park, Calif.: Addison-Wesley, 1982.

Graves, Donald. Donald Graves in Australia, *"Children Want to Write."* Exeter, N.H.: Heinemann Educational Books, 1982.

Hanna, Paul. *Sounds and Spelling in English.* Philadelphia: Chilton, 1971.

Jansky, J. "The Clinician in the Classroom: A First Grade Intervention Study." *Bulletin of the Orton Society* 31 (1981): 145–164.

Johnson, Doris J., and Helmer R. Myklebust. *Learning Disabilities: Educational Principle and Practices.* New York: Grune and Stratton, 1967.

Loan, Jim. "Denver Academy Math Curriculum." Unpublished manuscript, Denver Adacemy, 1982.

Loomer, Bradley M. *Educator's Guide to Spelling Research and Practice.* Iowa City, Iowa: Iowa State Department of Public Instruction, 1978.

Maurer, Richard. "Dropout Prevention: An Invervention Model for Today's High Schools." *Phi Delta Kappan* (March 1982): 470–471.

Reid, Kim D., and Wayne P. Hresko. *A Cognitive Approach to Learning Disabilities.* New York: McGraw-Hill, 1981.

SADCU: School Administrator's Discipline and Control Update. "Project Intercept: State-of-the-Art Discipline Program Prevents Pupil Suspensions." Waterford, Ct.: Croft-NEI, January, 1982.

Smith, Frank. *Reading Without Nonsense.* New York: Teachers College Press, 1978.

Spache, George D. *Diagnosing and Correcting Reading Disabilities.* Boston, Mass.: Allyn and Bacon, 1981.

Spache, George D., and Evelyn Spache. *Reading in the Elementary School.* Boston, Mass.: Allyn and Bacon, 1977.

Straw, Stanley. "Grammar and Teaching of Writing: Analysis Versus Synthesis," in *Research in the Language Arts.* Baltimore, Md.: University Park Press, 1981.

Tant, J. F., and V. I. Douglas. "Problem Solving in Hyperactive, Normal, and Reading-Disabled Boys." *Journal of Abnormal Child Psychology* 10, no. 3 (1982): 285–306.

Tattum, Stephan. "Structured Spelling Test." Unpublished manuscript, Denver Academy, 1982.

———. "Denver Academy Curriculum Guide." Unpublished manuscript, Denver Academy, 1983.

Thurstone, Thelma G. *Reading for Understanding.* Chicago, Ill.: Chicago Science Research Associates, 1978.

Tursman, Cindy. *Good Schools: What Makes Them Work.* Arlington, Va.: National School Public Relations Association, 1981.

White, Warren, and others. "Are There Learning Disabilities After High School?" *Exceptional Children* 49, no. 3 (1982): 273–274.

14

The Barat College Writing Lab

Dee C. Konrad

D URING THE SEVENTIES, writing labs mushroomed in American colleges and universities because many students entering those institutions lacked adequate writing skills. Storm signals flashed from that situation created a climate (both favorable and reluctant) that would sustain new or expanded facilities for developmental and/or remedial purposes. As the labs appeared, the harried halls of academe slowly shifted back to their "hallowed" reputation; but those halls were never to be the same. Administrators and faculty watched the changes, wondered about the total implication, and then evaluated both change and implication. Consequently, many of us who frequent academic halls view writing labs now not only as a distinctive response to a contemporary problem but also as a promise for the future. To supplement that current view, my specific topic, the establishment and maintenance of a writing lab, allows a brief review of the history of the Barat response to our students' writing problems: the Barat College Communication Skills Program and its lab, The Writing Place. The topic also permits a summary of the special activities of our program, an examination of the connection between our lab and the special program for our college-age learning-disabled students, and a quick look at the importance of that connection.

Barat College, a small, private liberal arts college in Lake Forest (a suburb north of Chicago) presented no exception early in the seventies to the national trend of a decline in writing skills. In 1974 the English Department focused attention on the disturbing fact that many current Barat students were less prepared for the demands of college writing than their predecessors. To counteract this lack of preparation, we established an English Center, one small room with one tutor, where students could go to improve their writing in a one-on-one meeting or in small groups. Some came voluntarily, others were referred. This was a small beginning, but an important one.

In 1977 our college received an AIDP grant that provided funds for several Barat programs. The provision for a Communication Skills Program enabled us to direct an all-out attack upon inadequate writing skills that in three years had become full-scale problems. We were empowered to redesign our writing courses, to develop new testing strategies, to add a reading component to our basic skills courses, and to expand the English Center into a broader operation—a writing lab.

The lab for the CSP was to be a major center for an assault upon weak communication skills. In preparation, faculty visited other writing labs, researched the literature, and attended conferences for additional ideas. For example, I have attended more than fifteen conferences or seminars on reading, writing, and the establishment and maintenance of writing labs, and I have visited five labs at other institutions.

A few special people and specific on-site visits provided stimulating ideas. One rewarding experience was at the University of California—Berkeley in a week-long seminar directed by Martha Maxwell. While there, we toured Thom Hawkins' writing lab—outstanding in the scope and implementation of its tutoring program that "services" the entire university. Attending "The Rites of Writing" at the University of Wisconsin, Stevens Point, was another beneficial experience. That event presented successful writers in a workshop setting. Donald M. Murray, of the University of New Hampshire, was one of those writers. Participants also visited the exceptional writing lab developed by Mary Croft. Maxwell, Hawkins, and Croft are experts. Two other experts on the subject of labs are JoyceSteward, of the University of Wisconsin, Madison, and Barbara Guenther, of the Chicago Art Institute. The counsel of these individuals is highly recommended.

But information and training were not enough for our expansion. We needed a larger home. Fortunately, we were given a small wing of the college, which gave us space for all types of writing. This new home, dubbed "The Write Wing," provided a large room for The Writing Place. Fresh paint, desks for tutors, lamps, reference books, comfortable old furniture found here and there, plants, posters, statements about writing placed on a bulletin board—and voila! In 1978 we were ready to open. Other rooms of the wing were assigned as writing faculty offices, seminar centers, and headquarters for the college literary publications.

The facility was crucial to our program, but so was the staff, which included both professional and peer tutors. Not all students selected for our staff were English majors, but all of them had excellent writing skills and warm, friendly personalities. Most tutors were and are paid through the Barat Work-Study Program. The training of tutors was both formal and informal. We experimented with a peer-tutoring course, team-taught by instructors from the Education and the English departments; but most training was on-going in private sessions with the Director of the CSP and her assistant. We also asked the staff to read about tutoring principles and techniques. One of the first books we used was *Errors and Expectations* by Mina Shaughnessy.

With space and staff, we now needed to advertise our existence. We held a reception for the faculty to explain the purpose of The Write Wing and The Writing Place. By special invitation, we enticed students, especially freshmen, to similar receptions. We used posters with lists of tutors and hours, sent letters and referral forms to faculty, and stuffed mailboxes with bookmarks that highlighted our message with quotations from famous writers. We also depended on the always-significant word of mouth.

When we opened the door of The Writing Place, we also opened a curricular door to our new Freshman Writing Program, another component of the CSP. We agreed that "writing is process" and committed ourselves to a program that stressed individualized attention. This agreement and commitment established a strong relationship between The Writing Place and the Freshman Writing Program. When freshman writers experienced difficulties, they were referred to the lab. Tutors worked with individual students or with small groups sent from their classrooms on a regular schedule. Writing Place staff offered workshops on topics such as "Sentence Sense," "Punctuation Puzzlers," or "How to Answer the Essay Question," which were open to the entire college community as well as to Freshmen.

The Writing Place has maintained its individualized attention to students who need and want to become better writers. We have logged hundreds of tutoring hours and have scheduled many workshops. Tutors work either with drop-ins or with students who have regularly scheduled appointments. Skilled writers seeking reassurance on organization or documentation, ESL students puzzled over prepositions, freshmen bewildered by a research paper assignment, continuing-education (re-entry) students straining for perfection, and learning disabled students—all move through the lab door with anxious pens. In response, tutors concentrate on principles of good writing; they discuss rules of grammar, punctuation, and syntax; and they explore the mysteries of the sentence and the paragraph. The tutors exhort and encourage. A second government grant enables us to offer tutoring time during evening hours for re-entry students who are on campus to develop professional effectiveness.

Not all our activities are in the lab itself. The professional tutors have visited classes in disciplines other than English to discuss, for example, how to organize the term paper or how to focus on a subject in order to find a thesis statement. Working in the dorm with their tutees has helped tutors extend The Writing Place activity. One enterprising tutor voluntarily arranged an informal conversational English seminar in her dorm with some Japanese students. She has now transferred the group to The Writing Place. By directing a sentence-combining lab that meets weekly, two other tutors have earned credit for College Apprentice Teaching.

We usually have three to five peer tutors of junior or senior rank and at least one professional tutor. They work from four to ten hours a week as their schedules permit. Our professional tutor in the evening is on campus Monday through Thursday for three hours each night.

With this review of the history and activities of The Writing Place, we can now examine the connection between our lab and the learning disabilities program. This connection has been surprisingly simple to make. What we had in place in the Communication Skills Program locked into the LD program like a matching puzzle piece.

First, the location of the wing itself, set off from a main corridor, gives a separateness that we treasure. The privacy issue is not a major one, but it is a bonus for a few reticent students who wish to keep the fact of their learning disabilities from becoming public knowledge. The Writing Place is frequently used for LD meetings or parties, and we welcome this use of the lab. Sometimes our privacy is a bonus for other students as well. Yet our separateness is *not* isolation.

Second, the total support system of the CSP and our emphasis on the individual are two obvious advantages for special students. Often, the LD students' introduction to the CSP is through their enrollment in the Freshman Writing Program, which offers Fundamentals of Grammar as the first course in a sequence of three. The workbook that I have written for the grammar course responds, in part, to the distinctive needs of the LD students and presents a simplified approach to grammar. Helping some students adjust to college English, the Fundamentals course is useful for them as a stepping stone to the composition courses. Tutors, as well as instructors, are familiar with the text and use it in special sessions when appropriate. We are pleased with the general reaction to the workbook and the results from its use.

We have other options for our students. One-credit adjunct labs for the writing courses, already established when the LD program began, serve the LD student. The students can also take advantage of one-credit minicourses that we offer: Increasing Word Competency and Proofreading. Reading Strategies and the Sentence-Combining Lab, two other offerings, are full-semester courses for one credit. The students also have access to our files of theory and exercise sheets for independent study or tutoring sessions.

Third and last, the Director of the Communication Skills Program sits, as a writing specialist, on the Internal Advisory Board of the LD program. This participation is important and productive. Furthermore, writing instructors usually meet weekly with the LD Program Director as well as with the LD tutors to discuss the progress and the needs of their students. In these meetings, specialists explain individual types of disorders and the students' processing deficits. These discussions contribute richly to an understanding of each student's profile and lead to the development of strategies that utilize not only the students' own written work but also additional course and lab lessons, extra conferences, and specific directions from the LD team.

Have we had to lower our standards in the Communication Skills Program to accommodate the LD student? Not really—but in the freshman writing courses, we have made a few, carefully limited adjustments. For example, some students have been given a longer testing period or private and/or oral tests in the lab. For one or two other students, we have set special goals and objectives (always in consultation with the LD team). The taping of vocabulary lists that students may use at their convenience is another modification. These adaptations, however, have not created even a small wave in the regular flow of daily activities.

With the concerted effort of two programs, what have we accomplished? That story really belongs to the LD faculty: Susan Vogel, Director, and Pamela Adelman, Assistant Director. From our records, however, Table 14.1 illustrates a few simple statistics about the first group of LD students.

Table 14.1
Sentence Structure Scores

ETS Descriptive Test of Language Skills Items: The complete sentence Subordination-coordination Modifiers Possible score: 35					
Student	Pre-test:	*Fall '80*	Post-test:	*December '80*	Post-test: *May '81*
A		14		16	23
B		21		18	No Score
C		21		24	28
D		22		22	30
E		30		27	27
F		14		16	24
G		22		21	25
H		No Score		19	26

helped both to describe our system and to express our belief that an established lab is not only important to the general student body but can also
be utilized advantageously by college-age learning disabled students. A lab
does not need expensive equipment or materials in order to supplement
the innate support system of any LD program. Overall, one of the most
important requirements for successful activity is a strong bond between
the lab programmers and the LD team.

Now that a few colleges and universities have welcomed LD students
into special programs, we see new opportunities developing for writing labs.
Of course, labs will continue to be strong auxiliaries for instructional programs that are offered to traditional populations, but labs can definitely
extend valuable support to LD students. Writing labs indeed have been
a contemporary response to writing problems; however, the future of these
writing centers promises an exciting extension of communication skills.

Invited Paper

Background on the
Canadian ACLD Definition Adopted by CACLD,
October 18, 1981

Barbara McElgunn

The term "learning disabilities" was embraced with relief by parents in 1963 when they were attempting to organize on a national basis. It was a term that focused on what seemed to be the primary problem of their children, and which, they hoped, would catapult the education community into solving it. These were children who eluded traditional categories of exceptionality.

As early as the nineteenth century, these children had come to the attention of three perceptive British physicians working with boys in the public school system. One of these, eye surgeon Dr. James Hinshelwood, attempted to correlate his knowledge of patients who had received cerebral insult through disease or trauma with the similar symptoms he saw in children with reading problems. In 1917 he published his monograph, *Congenital Word Blindness*. "Word blindness" is still used in England to refer to dyslexia.

In the early 1930s, the American psychiatrist Dr. Samuel Orton refused to accept the then-current belief that emotional maladjustment was the root of problems with reading and other learning. He noted, for example, that children with learning problems often displayed "mixed laterality" (laterality being the process by which a person develops an awareness

Editors' Note: In October 1982, the Canadian Association for Children with Learning Disabilities made a historic decision regarding a definition of learning disabilities. This decision came about after intensive study beginning in the early part of 1976 and involving Canadian leadership in government and universities, in the parent organizations, and in health-related agencies. Mrs. Barbara McElgunn was invited by the editors to prepare this timely and historic statement for inclusion in Volume 5 of *The Best of ACLD*. Mrs. McElgunn, a nurse and parent who worked for many years with Dr. Wilder Penfield, Director of the Montreal Neurological Institute, has been a long-time leader in attempting to conceptualize a satisfactory national definition for Canada. It is our hope that by including this important statement in this volume, stimulus will be given to the efforts of professional personnel in the United States of America and in other countries to conceptualize professionally honest and accurate statements about learning disabilities.

of the existence of two sides of the body, and ability to recognize these two sides as right and left), and suggested that the failure of one hemisphere of the brain to become dominant caused the disorder. Today, factors around hemispheric dominance are still considered in the field of learning disabilities.

Following World War I, an encephalitis epidemic left in its wake a number of cases of true brain damage, leading to the description of the disorganized and erratic behavior associated with hyperkinesis (hyperactivity). In 1947 German neurologist and psychiatrist Alfred Strauss described this syndrome in children, noting both perceptual and abstract reasoning deficits. His statement was based on twenty years of earlier work in Germany and in the United States by his colleague, Heinz Werner, and by other research associates. Although for a time hyperactivity was described as "Strauss Syndrome," the terms "brain damaged" and "brain injured" became prevalent in the literature.

In 1959, noting perceptual and learning similarities in patients with cerebral palsy and other neurological handicaps, researchers in the field proposed the term "cerebral dysfunction" to include the following syndromes: cerebral palsy (basically a neuromotor disorder), mental retardation (primarily an intellectual disorder), and the then "hyperkinetic behavior disorder" characterized by irritability, short attention span, purposeless activity, and poor school work in reading, arithmetic, and handwriting. "Perceptually handicapped" became another term used synonymously with learning disability in the early sixties.

In 1963 in the United States, under the chairmanship of American neurologist Dr. Richmond Paine, planning was begun for the establishment of a series of task forces to investigate learning disabilities, a field which, by that time, had attained particular prominence in education, medicine, psychology, and the language specialties. The pressure of parent groups for appropriate services was an added and possible key factor in the formation of the task forces.

Task Force 1, dealing primarily with terminology and identification, examined no fewer than thirty-eight terms used in the literature to describe these children. At this time the designation "minimal brain dysfunction" (disturbance or impairment of function) came to be accepted as representing what was seen as a milder or subclinical degree of organic brain dysfunction on the continuum of other cerebral dysfunctions such as cerebral palsy, epilepsy, autism, and mental retardation, and included the following definition:

> The term "minimal brain dysfunction syndrome" refers to children of near average, average, or above average general intelligence with certain learning

or behavioral disabilities ranging from mild to severe, which are associated with deviations of function of the central nervous system. These deviations may manifest themselves by various combinations of impairment in perception, conceptualization, language, memory, and control of attention, impulse, or motor function.

Similar symptoms may or may not complicate the problems of children with cerebral palsy, epilepsy, mental retardation, blindness, or deafness.

These aberrations may arise from genetic variations, biochemical irregularities, perinatal brain insults, or other illnesses or injuries sustained during the years which are critical for the development and maturation of the central nervous system, or from unknown causes.

The report of Task Force 2, published in 1969, agreed with Task Force 1 that "multidisciplinary communication requiring precise, descriptive nomenclature is *essential* for effective identification, assessment, and total management of these children," that is, it is absolutely imperative that parents, teachers, and all professionals concerned with these children be working from the same basis of understanding.

In 1967 the National Advisory Council on Handicapped Children developed the following definition, which became part of United States Public Law 91-320 and 94-142 mandating Special Education in the U.S. This law states:

> Children with specific learning disabilities exhibit a disorder in one or more of the basic psychological processes involved in understanding or using spoken or written languages. These can be manifested in disorders of listening, thinking, talking, reading, writing, spelling, or arithmetic. They include conditions which have been referred to as perceptual handicaps — brain injury, minimal brain dysfunction, dyslexia, developmental aphasia, etc. They do not include learning problems basically due to visual hearing, or motor handicaps, to mental retardation, emotional disturbance, or to environmental disadvantage.

Although the NACHC definition generated a great deal of activity in the field, it did not promote consensus because it referred only indirectly to etiological factors. This, and the many definitions for education that followed, described the children by exclusion, or on the basis of a discrepancy between academic potential and academic functioning. Certainly since 1968 the field of learning disabilities had been characterized by conflict and confusion, as the original focus of the term became blurred and the term "learning disability" stretched to include, in most minds, all children who were underachieving for any reason. On the other hand, it is very possible that this "exclusion clause" has had the effect of excluding from appropriate programs children with learning disabilities who have come from disadvantaged backgrounds. Often the learning problems of such children would be diagnosed only in terms of their deprived environment, and not looked at in the real context of physiological causes. Thus, learning disabilities have tended to become a middle-class phenomenon — while the child of the middle class would be diagnosed as having a learning disability, a child of the slums would automatically be considered deprived. Unfortunate also has been the designation of learning disabilities as solely an educational problem and not a medical or health problem.

The need for more precision was becoming apparent to the Canadian Association for Children with Learning Disabilities in 1976. Edward Polak's report to CACLD following his cross-Canada visits, identified the vagaries and confusion concerning *which* children, and how many; the delays in remediation which resulted when the child was required by definition to be a year or two behind his peers before he received help; the scattered and erratic direction of research and teacher training in this area, and the potentially devastating trend toward unplanned mainstreaming. The report recommended that CACLD should attempt to develop a well-described and clear definition of learning disabilities.

At an important three-day pre-conference session during the First National Conference on Learning Disabilities, held in Ottawa in 1977, the CACLD sponsored a study entitled, "Project Consensus: National Advisory Council on the Definition of Learning Disabilities." An invited position paper written by Dr. William M. Cruickshank of the University of Michigan was analyzed and discussed with Dr. Cruickshank by some of Canada's foremost professionals and government officials in this field.

The final definitional statement incorporated many of the suggestions for modifications and revisions recommended by council members. It is important to note that Dr. Cruickshank was the first to define learning disabilities in a diagnostic/etiological framework — that of neurophysiological dysfunction.

This definition promoted an important consensus among the membership of CACLD on a number of major areas; however, there was a lack of consensus on other significant areas. There ensued a lengthy period of communication and discussion across Canada which became an important process for CACLD. The National Task Force on Learning Disabilities, an intensive one-year review of services and attitudes in Canada pertaining to young people with learning disabilities, was launched in 1978. Once again it became clear during this investigation that the lack of a concise definition was a major stumbling block to progress in many areas. The Task Force Report noted that very little attention was being directed to prevention, health aspects, biomedical research, early screening and intervention, to the impact of learning disabilities on the family, or to the social and emotional welfare of the young adult. In large measure the result of what the members termed "The handicap of misunderstanding" arose out of a definition which was directed primarily to "learning," and only as it applied to the educational system.

Drs. Cohen, Shaywitz, and Cohen, in referring to this population in the *Journal of Paediatrics,* touched on another aspect of the problem; "Interpretation of the few clinical investigations has been hampered by the often imprecise definition of the children under investigation and by the frequent incorporation, and subsequent overlap of several diverse diagnostic groups." The same statement could be said to apply to large numbers of educational and psychological studies.

In 1979, a subcommittee on the definition was directed to further the definitional issue; their report to the CACLD Board of Directors recommended that following statement of principle: That the term "learning disabilities" be defined:

— to represent children and youth of potentially average, average, or above average intelligence,
— to distinguish this subset of the learning impaired population from others with other types of learning difficulties,
— to delineate the known/implied etiological basis for learning disabilities,
— to describe in general terms the major signs and symptoms observed; with special emphasis in early life,
— to focus attention toward prevention, identification, and understanding of their specific needs,
— to encourage research in medicine, pediatrics, biochemistry genetics, the neurosciences, education and social work.

In 1981, a position paper on definition was prepared by the National Joint Committee for Learning Disabilities (NJCLD), composed of the six major and concerned organizations in the U.S.— Association for Children and Adults with Learning Disabilities; American Speech-Language-Hearing Association; Division for Children with Communication Disorders, Council for Exceptional Children; Division for Children with Learning Disabilities, Council for Exceptional Children; International Reading Association; and The Orton Society. The NJCLD definition paralleled the position of the CACLD definition committee, and also met many of the definitional criteria adopted by the CACLD Board of Directors in March 1979. The

NJCLD paper noted: "The etiology of learning disabilities is not stated clearly within the current definition but is implied by a listing of terms and disorders." The NJCLD urged "that the disorders represented by the collective term 'learning disabilities' be understood as intrinsic to the individual and that the basis of the disorders be presumed to be due to central nervous system dysfunction." As well, the NJCLD position stated that learning disabilities are not the primary and direct result of other handicapping conditions and should not be so confused. However it was noted that LD could occur concomitantly with other handicapping conditions. This seemed to open an important diagnostic and educational door for children who are multihandicapped.

The Canadian ACLD sub-committee (Barbara McElgunn, Yude Henteleff, David Barnes) modified this definition, including the effects of such dysfunctions on behavior as well as upon learning; drawing attention to the preschool child; adding attention, memory, coordination, social competence, and emotional maturation to the list of areas of possible difficulty or delay; a statement about possible causes based on present knowledge; and recognition that central nervous system dysfunction can be demonstrated by diagnostic techniques such as computerized EEG and neuropsychology.

This definition was circulated to the provinces for comment and consideration. Sixteen submissions were received and considered, resulting in further changes to the order and the wording.

This final draft was approved and adopted by the CACLD Board of Directors in Moncton following the Third National Conference, October 18, 1981. It states:

> Learning disabilities is a generic term that refers to a heterogeneous group of disorders due to identifiable or inferred central nervous system dysfunction. Such disorders may be manifested by delays in early development and/or difficulties in any of the following areas: attention, memory, reasoning, coordination, communicating, reading, writing, spelling, calculation, social competence, and emotional maturation.
>
> Learning disabilities are intrinsic to the individual, and may affect learning and behavior in any individual, including those with potentially average, average, or above average intelligence.
>
> Learning disabilities are not due primarily to visual, hearing, or motor handicaps; to mental retardation, emotional disturbance, or environmental disadvantage; although they may occur concurrently with any of these.
>
> Learning disabilities may arise from genetic variations, biochemical factors, events in the pre to peri-natal period, or any other subsequent events resulting in neurological impairment."

REFERENCES

CACLD Five Year Development Program. "They Are Not Alone." Ottawa: CACLD, 1979.

Clements, Sam D. "Minimal Brain Dysfunction in Children: Terminology and Identification. Phase One of a Three-Phase Project." Washington, D.C.: U.S. Department of Health, Education, and Welfare, 1966.

Cruickshank, William M. "Learning Disabilities: A Definitional Statement." *Issues and Initiatives*. Ottawa: CACLD, 1979.

Levy, Harold B. "Minimal Brain Dysfunction/Specific Learning Disability: A Clinical Approach for the Primary Physician." *Southern Medical Journal* 69 (May 1976): 642–46.

McElgunn, Barbara. "The Invisible Handicap." In *A Different Understanding: Learning Disabilities*. Toronto: The Ontario Educational Communications Authority, 1981.

NJCLD Statement. "Learning Disabilities: Issues on Definition." *Perspectives on Dyslexia* 6, no. 1 (February 1981).

Paine, Richmond S., *et al.* "MBD in Children: Educational, Medical and Health Related Services. Phase Two of a Three-Phase Project." Washington, D.C.: U.S. Department of Health, Education, and Welfare, 1969.

Polak, Edward. "A View From the Bottom Up." Report for CACLD, 1977.

Report of the CACLD Definition Committee. "Minutes of the Annual Meeting of the Members of the Canadian Association for Children With Learning Disabilities" March 24, 1979.

Shaywitz, S. E., D. J. Cohen, and B. Shaywitz. "The Biochemical Basis of Minimal Brain Dysfunction." *Journal of Pediatrics* 92, no. 2 (February 1978).

EARLY ADOLESCENCE TO EARLY ADULTHOOD

was composed in 10-point Compugraphic Times Roman and leaded 2 points,
with display type in Times Roman by Metricomp;
printed by sheet-fed offset on 50-pound, acid-free Glatfelter Offset,
adhesive bound with 10-point Carolina cover,
by Wickersham Printing Company, Inc.;
and published by

SYRACUSE UNIVERSITY PRESS

SYRACUSE, NEW YORK 13210

WITHDRAWN